MW00368726

Build a Web Site ***Now!***

Microsoft®
Visual Web Developer™ 2005
Express Edition

PUBLISHED BY
Microsoft Press
A Division of Microsoft Corporation
One Microsoft Way
Redmond, Washington 98052-6399

Library of Congress Control Number 2005933641

Printed and bound in the United States of America.

1 2 3 4 5 6 7 8 9 QWT 9 8 7 6 5

Distributed in Canada by H.B. Fenn and Company Ltd.

A CIP catalogue record for this book is available from the British Library.

Microsoft Press books are available through booksellers and distributors worldwide. For further information about international editions, contact your local Microsoft Corporation offi ce or contact Microsoft Press International directly at fax (425) 936-7329. Visit our Web site at www.microsoft.com/learning/. Send comments to mspinput@microsoft.com.

Microsoft, Active Directory, FrontPage, Intellisense, Microsoft Press, MSDN, SharePoint, Visual Basic, Visual C#, Visual J#, Visual Studio, Visual Web Developer, Windows, and Windows Server are either registered trademarks or trademarks of Microsoft Corporation in the United States and/or other countries.

The example companies, organizations, products, domain names, e-mail addresses, logos, people, places, and events depicted herein are fictitious. No association with any real company, organization, product, domain name, e-mail address, logo, person, place, or event is intended or should be inferred.

This book expresses the author's views and opinions. The information contained in this book is provided with out any express, statutory, or implied warranties. Neither the authors, Microsoft Corporation, nor its resellers, or distributors will be held liable for any damages caused or alleged to be caused either directly or indirectly by this book.

Acquisitions Editor: Ben Ryan
Project Editor: Sandra Haynes
Editorial and Production: Custom Editorial Productions, Inc.

Body Part No. X11-50125

Contents

Introduction

Congratulations on your interest in Microsoft Visual Web Developer 2005 Express Edition. This exciting new software brings two of Microsoft's most powerful technologies—ASP.NET 2.0 and Visual Studio 2005—within reach of anyone who creates Web sites.

Visual Web Developer is a fully functional subset of Visual Studio 2005 suitable for creating and maintaining a wide range of Web sites over time. It's certainly not a crippled or limited time demo version. Instead, it's a key Microsoft initiative for bringing the power of Visual Studio and ASP.NET not only to professional programmers, but to hobbyists and entrepreneurs as well.

Who Is This Book For?

This book is primarily for people who've already designed and deployed a Web site or two, but found the process or the tools limiting. For example, they may have found features such as these difficult to implement:

- Reliable, reusable, and active page templates and page segments.

- Easy-to-use dynamic menus, expandable tree views, or breadcrumbs.

- Fast, flexible, and easy ways of working with databases.

- Controlled access to portions of a site, with or without self-registration.

ASP.NET 2.0 has built-in controls that provide these features and yet, in many cases, require no program code at all.

What's more, you can add and configure these controls entirely through Visual Web Developer's graphical interface. Visual Web Developer, like Visual Studio, has world class editors for graphical design and for working with code of all kinds. Its features for working with HTML, CSS, and XML are no less than its power for working with sophisticated program code.

If this is the kind of power you crave, or if you're ready to advance from legacy ASP to ASP.NET and need a place to get started, this is the book for you.

How This Book Is Organized

The book consists of sixteen chapters plus two bonus chapters on the companion Web site. (See "Bonus Material" below.) Although each chapter describes a specific technology or feature, the exercises do build on skills and results from earlier in the book. As a result, you should plan on reading the material sequentially.

Bonus Material

Two additional chapters, Chapter 17, *Controlling Access to Your Site* and Chapter 18, *Displaying Web Parts,* are provided on the companion Web site at *http://www.microsoft.com/mspress/companion/0-7356-2212-4/.*

Conventions and Features in This Book

This book presents information using conventions designed to make the information readable and easy to follow. Before you start the book, read the following list, which explains conventions you'll see throughout the book and points out helpful features in the book that you might want to use.

Conventions

- Each exercise is a series of tasks. Each task is presented as a series of numbered steps (1, 2, and so on). Each exercise is preceded by a procedural heading that lets you know what you will accomplish in the exercise.

- Notes labeled "Tip" provide additional information or alternative methods for completing a step successfully.

- Notes labeled "Caution" alert you to information you need to check before continuing.

- Text that you type or items you select or click appear in bold.

- Menu commands, dialog box titles, and other user interface elements appear with each word capitalized.

- A plus sign (+) between two key names means that you must press those keys at the same time. For example, "Press Alt+Tab" means that you hold down the Alt key while you press the Tab key.

Other Features

- Shaded sidebars throughout the book provide more in-depth information about the content. The sidebars might contain background information, design tips, or features related to the information being discussed.

- Each chapter ends with an In Summary... section that briefly reviews what you learned in the current chapter and previews what the next chapter will present.

System Requirements

You'll need the following hardware and software to complete the exercises in this book:

- Microsoft Windows XP with Service Pack 2, Microsoft Windows Server 2003 with Service Pack 1, or Microsoft Windows 2000 with Service Pack 4

- Microsoft Visual Web Developer 2005 Express Edition

- PC with a Pentium III-class processor, 600 MHz Recommended: 1 GHz

- 128 MB RAM (256 MB or more recommended)

- 16.4 MB hard disk space for sample files

- Video (800 x 600 or higher resolution) monitor with at least 256 colors (1024 x 768 High Color 16-bit recommended)

- CD-ROM or DVD-ROM drive

- Microsoft Mouse or compatible pointing device

You'll also need administrator access to your computer to configure SQL Server 2005 Express.

NOTE
The CD-ROM packaged in the back of this book contains the Visual Web Developer 2005 Express Edition software needed to complete the exercises in this book.

Obtaining the Sample Web Site

To obtain a sample Web site incorporating the examples, browse the book's companion content page at the following address:

http://www.microsoft.com/mspress/companion/0-7356-2212-4/

To download and install this site, follow the procedure titled, "To Obtain And Install the Sample Files For This Book," in Chapter 1.

Running the Exercises and Sample Web Site

ASP.NET is a technology that runs primarily on a Web sever. You'll need a Web server to test and run the examples in each chapter, and of course the completed sample Web site.

Fortunately, Visual Web Developer comes with its own integrated Development Web Server. Both the exercises and the completed sample Web site presume you'll be using this facility. Therefore, there's no need to install or access a full copy of Internet Information Server (IIS).

NOTE
Visual Web Developer's built-in Web server is accessible only from the local computer. Any server that delivers the finished Web site will need a full copy of IIS.

NOTE

Although you can develop Web sites using SQL Server 2005 Express Edition, you, your IT department, or your host will need a full copy of SQL Server for delivering the site to visitors.

The exercises in Chapters 13 through 16 (and Chapters 17 and 18 on the companion site) require that SQL Server 2005 Express Edition (or SQL Server 2005) be installed on the same computer as Visual Web Developer. If you install your software from the Companion CD, this will be the default. Because the exercises and sample Web site use a new SQL Server 2005 feature called *user instancing*, no special security configuration is necessary.

Removing the Sample Web Site

To remove the sample Web site from your computer, follow these steps:

1 In Control Panel, open **Add Or Remove Programs**.

2 From the list of Currently Installed Programs, select **Microsoft Visual Web Developer 2005 Express Edition: Build A Web Site Now!**

3 Click **Remove**.

4 Follow any further instructions that appear.

Prerelease Software

This book was reviewed and tested against the August 2005 Community Technical Preview (CTP) of Visual Studio 2005. The August CTP was the last preview before the final release of Visual Studio 2005. This book is expected to be fully compatible with the final release of Visual Studio 2005. If there are any changes or corrections for this book, they'll be collected and added to a Microsoft Knowledge Base article. See the "Support for this Book" section in this Introduction for more information.

Technology Updates

As technologies related to this book are updated, links to additional information will be added to the Microsoft Press Technology Updates Web page. Visit this page periodically for updates on Visual Studio 2005 and other technologies.

http://www.microsoft.com/mspress/updates/

Support for This Book

Every effort has been made to ensure the accuracy of this book and the companion content. As corrections or changes are collected, they'll be added to a Microsoft Knowledge Base article. To view the list of known corrections for this book, visit the following article:

http://support.microsoft.com/kb/905041

Microsoft Press provides support for books and companion content at the following Web site:

http://www.microsoft.com/learning/support/books/

Questions and Comments

If you have comments, questions, or ideas regarding the book or the companion content, or questions that are not answered by visiting the sites above, please send them to Microsoft Press via e-mail to

mspinput@microsoft.com

or via postal mail to

Microsoft Press
Attn: Visual Web Developer 2005 Express Edition Build a Web Site Now Editor
One Microsoft Way
Redmond, WA 98052-6399

Please note that Microsoft offers no software product support through these addresses.

Jim Buyens

Jim Buyens has been professionally involved with the World Wide Web since its inception, including roles as a server administrator, Web master, content developer, system developer, and system architect. He has many years of experience in the telecommunications industry, and is also an acclaimed Microsoft Most Valuable Professional (MVP) who contributes extensively to the Microsoft Online FrontPage Communities.

Jim received a Bachelor of Science degree in Computer Science from Purdue University in 1971 and a Master of Business Administration from Arizona State University in 1992. When not enhancing the Web or writing books, he enjoys traveling and attending professional sports events—especially NHL hockey. He resides with his family in Phoenix.

Other books by Jim Buyens include:

- Microsoft Windows SharePoint Services Inside Out, March, 2005, Microsoft Press

- Microsoft Office FrontPage Version 2003 Inside Out, August, 2003, Microsoft Press

- Faster Smarter Beginning Programming, November, 2002, Microsoft Press

- Web Database Development Step by Step .NET Edition, June, 2002, Microsoft Press

- Troubleshooting Microsoft FrontPage 2002, May, 2002, Microsoft Press

- Microsoft FrontPage Version 2002 Inside Out, May, 2001, Microsoft Press

- Web Database Development Step by Step, June, 2000, Microsoft Press

- Running Microsoft FrontPage 2000, June, 1999, Microsoft Press

- Stupid Web Tricks, July, 1998, Microsoft Press

- Running Microsoft FrontPage 98, October, 1997, Microsoft Press

- Building Net Sites with Windows NT—An Internet Services Handbook, July 1996, Addison-Wesley Developers Press

Dedication

This book is dedicated to the homeless mentally-ill persons of America. Why do we lavish health care dollars on victims of other, less debilitating illnesses while condemning these unfortunates to the streets and gutters?

Chapter 1

Introducing Microsoft® Visual Web Developer™ 2005 Express Edition

Congratulations on your interest in Microsoft Visual Web Developer Express Edition. This incredible software makes it very easy for hobbyists, enthusiasts, and non-professional Web developers to start using Microsoft ASP.NET 2.0, the world's premier technology for creating and running Web sites.

Does the idea of using ASP.NET scare you? Well, with the arrival of ASP.NET 2.0, it needn't. Although release 2.0 has many enhancements targeted primarily at professional programmers, it also provides simple and elegant ways of implementing some of the most challenging yet popular features on the Web—without requiring a single line of program code! For example, you can:

- Create dynamic drop-down or fly-out menus.

- Surround the variable content on each page with dynamic content from a so-called *master page*.

- Code a site map once and then use it to create menus and breadcrumb trails on each page.

- Query, create, update, and delete database records.

- Close portions of your site except to registered visitors.

- Let individual visitors customize the way they view your site. This includes not only the site's visual appearance but also—to the extent you want— the layout and content of specific pages.

Although none of this requires any program code, it does require adding some special XML tags to your Web pages. But even here, Microsoft keeps things simple. With Visual Web Developer you can implement many ASP.NET features (generally the most popular ones) in pure graphical design view. That means no looking at HTML, no looking at obscure XML tags, and certainly no looking at program code.

Of course, if you want to look at (or even write!) HTML code, XML code, or program code, Visual Web Developer provides great ways of doing just that. Because it's based on Microsoft Visual Studio® 2005—the premier environment for professional programmers—Visual Web Developer Express comes with the largest, most powerful, and easiest-to-use selection of code editors you're likely to find anywhere. And yes, if you start a project in Visual Web Developer, you can continue it in products like Microsoft Visual Basic® .NET Standard Edition, Microsoft C# Standard Edition, or any of the full Visual Studio products.

What to Expect From This Book

This book assumes you're already familiar with the basic workings of the World Wide Web and with some typical Windows applications such as Microsoft Office. For example, it assumes you know how to create ordinary ("flat") HTML pages and link them into a Web site.

Even though Visual Web Developer is a subset of Visual Studio 2005 (a sophisticated programming tool) the book also assumes that you *don't* want to write your own HTML, XML, or program code. Instead, the book explains how to get professional ASP.NET 2.0 results using only the graphical Web page editor.

If you *do* want to write your own code, rest assured that the book *will* show you how to view and modify the code that the graphical interface creates. The details of any code you write, however, will be up to you. If you want to learn about the Visual Basic .NET, C#, or J# programming languages, about ASP.NET, or about the .NET framework in general, you'll need to find a separate book on the topic you want, or explore the online information at *http://msdn.microsoft.com*.

Finally, the book will concentrate on using features new to ASP.NET 2.0. Presumably, these are the features that attracted you to Visual Web Developer in the first place. As to the older features, the procedures for using them are about the same as for the newer ones. Once you understand using the new features, using the older ones should be fairly intuitive.

Deciding Whether Visual Web Developer is the Product for You

Microsoft designed Visual Web Developer specifically for non-professional programmers who want to develop Web sites that use the features of ASP.NET 2.0. If this is your situation, Visual Web Developer is the product for you.

Of course, no one product can be best for all people, and in all situations. Here are some scenarios where other products might be a better choice:

- In theory, you could use Visual Web Developer to create Web sites that don't use any ASP.NET features. That is, you could use it strictly as an HTML editor. This, however, forgoes the strong points of the product. If all you want is an HTML editor, you might prefer a simpler product dedicated to that task.

- In theory, you could also use Visual Web Developer to create ASP.NET 1.1 Web sites. This, however, would be difficult because Visual Web Developer won't stop you from using the new features in ASP.NET 2.0. If you need to build Web sites that use ASP.NET 1.1, you'll probably find it easier to use Microsoft Visual Studio 2003 or Microsoft ASP.NET Web Matrix.

- Visual Web Developer can't create Windows desktop applications. If you need to create Windows applications, obtain the 2005 Express Edition of Visual Basic, C#, C++, or J#, graduate to the Standard version of those languages, or invest in a full version of Visual Studio.

Further Reading

To learn more about ASP.NET 2.0, C#, Visual Basic .NET, or SQL Server™ Express, consider these books from Microsoft Press®:

- *Microsoft Visual C#® 2005 Express Edition: Build a Program Now!, by Patrice Pelland*
- *Microsoft ASP.NET 2.0 Programming Step By Step, by George Shepherd*
- *Microsoft Visual Basic 2005 Step by Step, by Michael Halvorson*
- *Microsoft Visual C# 2005 Step by Step, by John Sharp*
- *Developing Database Applications with Microsoft SQL Server 2005 Express Step by Step, by Jackie Goldstein*

- Professional and expert programmers are likely to need the high-end tools and features that full versions of Visual Studio provide. For example, Microsoft Visual Studio 2005 Professional Edition can create many more kinds of software, and Microsoft Visual Studio 2005 Team System has special features that support teams of software developers working on the same project.

What You'll Need for Testing

Although it creates HTML, CSS, and JavaScript code that runs on the browser, ASP.NET is primarily a server-side technology. It:

1. Reads Web pages and other files from the Web server's file system.
2. Runs program code to access server-based resources and modify the current Web page.
3. Sends the modified Web page to the visitor.

As a result, to test an ASP.NET page you really need a Web server. If you have Microsoft Internet Information Server (IIS, Microsoft's premier Web server) and ASP.NET 2.0 installed on your PC, you can certainly use those resources for testing. But if you don't, Visual Web Developer will use its own built-in mini-Web server. Visual Web Developer starts this Web server the first time you browse or debug a page, and stops it when you quit Visual Web Developer.

Visual Web Developer fully supports one and only one type of database: Microsoft SQL Server. If the prospect of using SQL Server seems daunting, consider these facts:

- Visual Web Developer has full built-in graphical support for creating, viewing, modifying, and deleting SQL Server databases, tables, and fields. As a result, you can perform these tasks without using external programs such as Microsoft SQL Enterprise Manager or Microsoft Access.

- You don't need to buy a copy of SQL Server for your own PC. SQL Server 2005 Express Edition is perfectly sufficient for developing your Web site, and it's a free download.

Microsoft has made SQL Server databases as easy to upload as Access databases. The entire SQL Server database resides in one file (with a .dbf filename extension) that you can upload to your hosting provider. In many cases, simply browsing your Web site will then *attach* your database (that, is make it available) to the copy of SQL Server that services your site. Providers who don't support this feature can initially attach the database for you.

Choosing a Provider for Your Public Web Site

Although Visual Web Developer includes its own Web server, and although SQL Server 2005 Express is perfectly adequate for development and testing, your production Web site will need full copies of:

- Microsoft Windows® 2000 Server or Microsoft Windows Server™ 2003.
- IIS.
- ASP.NET 2.0.
- Microsoft SQL Server 2000 or Microsoft SQL Server 2005.

If your current hosting provider can't supply all these capabilities, you'll probably need to find a new provider. One place to look for a new provider is the Hosters Providing ASP.NET page at:

http://msdn.microsoft.com/asp.net/info/hosters/default.aspx

The following sites may also be useful when searching for an ASP.NET 2.0 hosting provider:

- Locate a Web Presence Provider (Microsoft FrontPage®)
  http://www.microsoft.com/office/frontpage/prodinfo/partner/wpp.asp
- Windows Host List (Automation Tools, LLC)
  http://www.windowshostlist.com/hostlist.aspx
- Web Hosting Resource and Directory (Affinity Internet Inc.)
  http://www.tophosts.com/

What about ASP.NET Web Matrix?

ASP.NET Web Matrix is an unsupported tool that Microsoft released to help evaluators, hobbyists, and enthusiasts get started building ASP.NET 1.0 and 1.1 applications. It has no direct relationship to any Visual Studio product.

Visual Web Developer, by contrast, is a direct member of the Visual Studio 2005 family. As a result, much of the support, attention, and advice you find for Visual Studio will apply to Visual Web Developer as well.

During development, Microsoft integrated many of the lessons learned, feedback, and top features from ASP.NET Web Matrix into Visual Web Developer.

- WHT Host Quote (WebHostingTalk.Com)
  http://www.webhostingtalk.com/request.php

You can, of course, search for a hosting provider any way you like. Microsoft intends to work with hosting providers so that every Web developer or business can afford an ASP.NET 2.0 Web site enhanced with SQL Server.

OBTAINING AND INSTALLING VISUAL WEB DEVELOPER

1 If you have a CD that contains the setup files for Visual Web Developer, put it in your CD drive and wait for the splash screen to appear. Otherwise, browse http://msdn.microsoft.com/downloads/, search for Visual Web Developer Express, download the setup program, and run it.

2 Advance through the Installation Wizard's usual licensing and information screens. Eventually, an Installation Options page like the one in Figure 1-1 will appear.

3 Your setup options may vary depending on the version of Visual Web Developer you have, and depending on other software installed on your computer. With this in mind, use the guidelines on the next page to select the options you need:

4 Click the Next button to complete the installation.

IMPORTANT

You can run any combination of conventional HTML, ASP, ASP.NET 1.0, ASP.NET 1.1, and ASP.NET 2.0 applications on the same virtual Web server. If a particular application isn't running under the version of ASP.NET you want, an administrator can flag the application to run under the correct version.

Figure 1-1
The Start page appears when you open Visual Web Developer.

Microsoft MSDN 2005 Express Edition contains extensive help and other information about ASP.NET 2.0 and all the Express products. You should almost certainly install this option.

Microsoft SQL Server 2005 Express Edition provides a limited version of SQL Server 2005 that you can use for developing your Web site. Unless you have (or plan to have) a full version of SQL Server 2005 running on your PC, you should install this option.

Dealing with ISO Image Files

If you download any of the Visual Studio 2005 Express products and receive a file with an .iso or .img filename extension, the file is an *ISO image file*. Such files contain the exact representation of a CD or DVD.

- To copy an ISO image file to a recordable CD, use a utility such as ISORecorder, Nero, or Roxio.
- To extract an ISO image to a folder on your disk, use a utility such as ISObuster or DaemonTools.
- To map the ISO image onto an unused drive letter, use the Virtual CD-ROM Control Panel for Windows XP. To obtain this software by free download, refer to the FAQ page cited below.

For more information on using these products:

- Browse the MSDN® Subscriptions Frequently Asked Questions page at *http://msdn.microsoft.com/subscriptions/faq/default.aspx*
- Click MSDN Subscriber Downloads.
- Click the question, "What are ISO image files and how do I use them?"

TO OBTAIN AND INSTALL THE SAMPLE FILES FOR THIS BOOK

The examples and exercises in this book involve an imaginary Web site for Contoso Magic, an illusory supply shop for stage magicians. To install the completed Web site and databases on your computer:

1 Install Visual Web Developer and a compatible version of SQL Server as the previous section instructed.

2 Download the setup program from *http://www.microsoft.com/mspress/companion/0-7356-2212-4/*.

3 Run the downloaded setup program to install the sample files at My Documents\Microsoft Press\Visual Web Developer. The My Documents folder usually resides at C:\Documents and Settings\<username>\My Documents.

4 To open the finished Web site for Chapters 1-16, start Visual Web Developer, choose Open Web Site from the file menu, and specify the site location as My Documents\Microsoft Press\Visual Web Developer\ContosoMagic.

To open the finished Web site for the entire book (including Chapters 17 and 18), specify the site location as:
My Documents\Microsoft Press\Visual Web Developer\ContosoMagic17

Approaching the User Interface

The first time you start Visual Web Developer, a display like the one in Figure 1-2 will appear. Because no project (that is, no Web site) is open, many of the frames and controls are dimmed. Nevertheless, here's a brief rundown of those that appear by default:

■ The menu bar and toolbars work exactly like those in Microsoft Office and other Microsoft programs. Of course, the commands are suited to Web site development, and not to word processing or spreadsheets.

■ The Toolbox frame at the left will contain objects that you can drag onto an open Web page. Of course, this requires that both a project and a Web page be open.

■ The Start Page in the center displays a list of projects you recently opened, a list of templates you can use for starting new projects, and some links to useful Web pages on Microsoft's Web site.

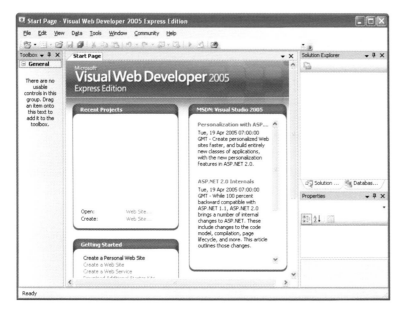

Figure 1-2
Opening a project reveals the full
power of Visual Web Developer.

■ The Solution Explorer at the right will display a list of the files and folders in an open project.

■ A Database Explorer frame is tabbed behind the Solution Explorer frame. This is where you'll create, modify, and delete databases, tables, and fields.

■ The Properties frame will display an editable list of available properties and current settings for any object you select while, for example, editing a Web page.

The menu bar, the toolbars, and all the frames are dockable. That means you can drag them away from their current positions along the window border, park them along another border, or leave them floating. Again, this works just like dockable frames in Microsoft Office.

Figure 1-3 shows how Visual Web Developer looks when a project is open. The toolbox now shows a selection of controls; the center of the window displays an open Web page ready for editing; the Solution Explorer shows the files and folders in the project, and the Properties frame shows the properties and values for the current element (which happens to be the entire document).

The page in the figure makes use of these ASP.NET 2.0 features:

- The top, left, and bottom edges of the Web page are dimmed because they come from a *master page*: in other words, from a template file that many other pages can incorporate to ensure uniformity. Chapter 9 will explain master pages.

The master page in the figure includes these ASP.NET elements:

- The area that displays [Literal "litBannerTitle"] is an ASP.NET *Literal* control. One line of program code retrieves the title of the current page and copies it into the area where this control resides. Chapter 9 will explain this technique.

- The menu items Home, Products, and Services are the top-level choices in a fly-out menu built automatically from a site map file. Chapter 12 explains menus and site map files.

- The *SiteMapDataSource* control provides database-like access to the site map file. Chapter 12 explains these, too.

- The *[UserName]* control shows the name of the currently-logged-in user. Chapter 17 will provide more information about this control.

- The *Login* control generates a link to a page where visitors can log in or self-register. Chapter 17 explains how this works.

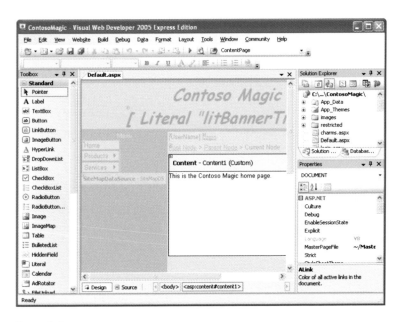

Figure 1–3
Opening a project reveals the full power of Visual Web Developer.

- The area displaying root Node > Parent Node > Current Node is a *SiteMapPath* control. This control looks in the site map file, finds the URL of the current page, and displays a series of links back to the home page. For more information about this, consult Chapter 12.

- The control titled *Content - Content1 (Custom)* marks an area that the Master Page leaves open for the content of individual pages. Chapter 12 explains how this works.

- The sentence, "This is the Contoso Magic home page," is variable content unique to the Default.aspx page.

If this example seems overly controlled—with so much content coming from a master page—keep in mind that the designer *chooses* to work this way. There's no requirement to use master pages at all, and no requirement to use any of the other controls shown in the figure. However, this page does illustrate the power that ASP.NET 2.0 delivers to non-programmers. Consider:

- The site map file consists of simple, highly-repetitive XML statements like this:
  <siteMapNode url="default.aspx" title="Home page" />

- The Master Page contains one line of program code, the one that copies the page title into the page banner.

- Other than these two items, you can create this entire page (or site) without ever leaving the Visual Web Developer graphical interface.

In Summary...

Visual Web Developer is a powerful tool with a simple graphical interface that non-programmers and beginners can use to create ASP.NET 2.0 Web sites.

Chapter 2 will explain the essentials of ASP.NET.

Chapter 2

Presenting the ASP.NET 2.0 Programming Model

ASP.NET is a major component of Microsoft's overall .NET initiative. Compared to earlier technologies like Microsoft® Active Server Pages (ASP) and PHP Hypertext Processor (PHP), ASP.NET is much broader, much more powerful, and much more robust. Because of these improvements in ASP. NET, Microsoft has designated Active Server Pages as a legacy technology that will eventually disappear.

Compared to earlier versions, ASP.NET 2.0 provides many improvements in both power and ease of use. Nevertheless, all versions of ASP.NET deliver Web pages in about the same way. The next section will explain how this works. Later, another section will describe the basic types of ASP.NET software components you can add to a Web page.

Keep in mind that this chapter is only a brief introduction to these topics. Entire books have been written about them. The material in this chapter is only enough to get you started with Microsoft Visual Web Developer™.

If even this introduction seems a bit abstract or difficult, just skip ahead to Chapter 3. You can always refer back later.

For the most part, ASP.NET runs on a Web server. Each time a Web visitor requests a page that has an ASP.NET file name extension, such as .aspx, ASP.NET:

1. Loads the requested page into the Web server's memory.

2. Executes any ASP.NET software components that the Web page contains.

3. Sends the resulting page to the Web visitor.

When loading a Web page into memory, ASP.NET differentiates between two very different kinds of content.

■ **Ordinary HTML Tags** are just that: ordinary HTML. ASP.NET does nothing with these, except to store them and later transmit them exactly "as is." If, for example, your page contained this tag:

```
<img src="images/mylogo.gif">
```

then ASP.NET would send

```
<img src="images/mylogo.gif">
```

to the Web visitors. The Web server doesn't change ordinary HTML at all.

■ **ASP.NET Server Controls** are software components that ASP.NET loads into memory. The following tag, for example, tells ASP.NET to load an *HtmlImage* server control into memory.

```
<img src="images/mylogo.gif" id="imgMyLogo" runat="server" />
```

The most important difference between this tag and the previous one is the *runat="server"* attribute, which tells ASP.NET to create a server control on the Web server. In addition:

■ The tag name (*img* in this case) tells ASP.NET what kind of server control to create.

■ The *id=* attribute provides a name to which other server controls in the same page can refer.

- ASP.NET passes the *src=* attribute (and any others that may be present) to the server control as input.

- The trailing slash satisfies the XML requirement for an end tag.

Once ASP.NET finishes loading a server control, it discards the XML that created it. When it's time to send the page to the visitor, ASP.NET *doesn't* send the server control's original XML tag. Instead, it calls a function (or more correctly, a *method*) named *Render* that's part of the server control, and then, it sends the output of that method to the Web visitor.

Although all the server controls that come with ASP.NET 2.0 render their output as HTML, ASP.NET enforces no restrictions on the output of a server control's *Render* method. The output doesn't have to resemble the original XML tag, and doesn't even have to be HTML. For example, it could be a picture file or a Microsoft Word document.

To summarize the life cycle of an ASP.NET page:

NOTE

Every ASP.NET server control has a *Render* method.

1. A visitor requests a file having an .aspx extension.

2. ASP.NET reads the file from the server's file system.

3. ASP.NET inspects each tag in the file and loads it into memory.

   - If the tag contains a *runat="server"* attribute, ASP.NET loads a software component called a server control. The tag name determines the type of server control.

   - Tags with no *runat="server"* attribute are ordinary HTML. ASP.NET loads these into a software component that will, at the proper time, send the original tag to the Web visitor verbatim.

4. After loading all the tags into memory, ASP.NET executes designated program code within each server control. This code can access resources on the Web server; it can change the content or properties of any server control on the page; and it can even add or remove other server controls.

TIP

ASP.NET treats all server control tags as XML, and therefore requires them to have end tags. If you don't want to code an explicit end tag, as in

```
<img src="myphoto.jpg" runat="server"></img>
```

code a slash before the closing angle bracket like this:

```
<img src="myphoto.jpg" runat="server" />
```

5. When all the code in all the server controls finishes executing (that is, when the entire stack of server controls comes to rest) ASP.NET sequentially tells each control to *render* itself (that is, to supply whatever HTML the visitor should receive).

  ▪ If the original tag was ordinary HTML, ASP.NET sends it without modification.

  ▪ If the original tag created a server control, ASP.NET calls the control's *Render* method to generate the HTML the Web visitor should receive.

6. Once the page has left the server, ASP.NET releases its server controls and any other resources it may have created.

A Hierarchy of Controls

When ASP.NET loads server controls into memory, it doesn't store them as a "flat" list. Instead, it stores them in a hierarchical tree. This approach is quite ingenious, and it illustrates the power of ASP.NET.

Every server control has a *Controls* collection capable of holding additional server controls. In fact, the ASP.NET page itself is a server control: a *Page* server control. The *Page* control uses its *Controls* collection to store a list of additional server controls. Each of those controls has its own *Controls* collection that can store more server controls, and so forth.

This hierarchy of controls is useful in situations like that shown in the following code. A *<table>* tag contains two *<tr>* tags, and the *<tr>* tags each contain *<td>* tags.

```
<table id="tblPlenty" runat="server">
  <tr id="rowPlentyHeading" runat="server">
    <td colspan="3" id="celPlentyTitle" runat="server"></td>
  </tr>
  <tr id="rowPlentyDetail" runat="server">
    <td id="celPlentyAmount" runat="server"></td>
    <td id="celPlentyUnit" runat="server"></td>
    <td id="celPlentyDescription" runat="server"></td>
  </tr>
</table>
```

Presumably, all this code would exist within a Web page. The top of the hierarchy would therefore be a *Page* control. From that point:

- The *Controls* collection in the Page server control would contain the *HtmlTable* server control named *tblPlenty*.

- The *Controls* collection in the HtmlTable server control would contain two *HtmlTableRow* server controls: *rowPlentyHeading* and *rowPlentyDetail*.

- The *HtmlTableRow* server control named *rowPlentyHeading* would have one item in its Controls collection: the *HtmlTableCell* server control named *celPlentyTitle*.

- The *HtmlTableRow* server control named *rowPlentyDetail* would have three items in its Controls collection: the *HtmlTableCell* server controls named *celPlentyAmount*, *celPlentyUnit*, and *celPlentyDescription*.

  When ASP.NET tells the page to render itself:

- The *Page* control tells each member in its *Controls* collection to render itself at the proper time. In this example, the *Page* control would tell the *tblPlenty* server control to render itself.

- Each control (such as *tblPlenty*) that has subordinate controls tells those subordinates to render themselves. For example, the *tblPlenty* control would tell the *rowPlentyHeading* and *rowPlentyDetail* controls to render themselves.

- Likewise, the *rowPlentyHeading* would tell the *celPlentyTitle* control to render itself and finally the *rowPlentyDetail* control would tell the *celPlentyAmount*, *celPlentyUnit*, and *celPlentyDescription* controls to render themselves.

Program code can manipulate server controls, create new ones, and delete any that aren't appropriate to a particular request. For example, after retrieving one row from a database query, program code could create an *HtmlTableRow* object, append an *HtmlTableCell* object to display each output field, and then append the *HtmlTableRow* object to the existing table.

Dealing with Events

ASP.NET server controls have a fleeting existence. The whole life cycle of reading, executing, and transmitting an ASP.NET page consumes only fractions of a second: milliseconds or less.

Nevertheless, during that fraction of a second, ASP.NET bombards each server control with a series of messages called *events*. For each event, a given server control may or may not have a matching *event handler* (which is a kind of function or subroutine). If a handler is present, ASP.NET will run it whenever the given event occurs.

ASP.NET raises up to 30 events for each server control in a page. Fortunately, most programmers, even advanced ones, seldom need to worry about all these events. Table 2-1 lists the events that Web developers use the most.

Table 2-1
Common Server Control Events

Event	Occurs When
OnInit	ASP.NET initializes the server control.
OnLoad	ASP.NET finishes loading the server control.
OnPreRender	ASP.NET is ready to start asking server controls to render themselves.
OnUnload	ASP.NET is about to remove the server control from memory.

Among these events, the *Page* object's *OnLoad* event is probably the most useful. This event occurs when ASP.NET has finished loading all the page's server controls into memory, but before ASP.NET has begun sending the Web page to the visitor. This usually is the perfect time to perform whatever processing the page requires.

Some ASP.NET server controls generate server-based events in response to actions that take place on the browser. For example, clicking a button or changing the selection in a drop-down list can:

- Initiate a request to the Web server.
- Re-execute the same page.

- Raise a special event that reflects the button click or change of selection.

- Run a custom-written event handler that performs whatever processing the event requires.

The fact that ASP.NET wires each significant browser event to a different server-side event handler is a great feature. It truly simplifies the task of ensuring that the right code runs in response to each event.

Reviewing the Page Life Cycle

This section introduced the life cycle of an ASP.NET page as it passes through the Web server. Incorporating all the details, here's how this works:

- ASP.NET first retrieves the page from the server's file system and loads it into memory. If a tag contains a *runat="server"* attribute, ASP.NET loads a corresponding server control. Otherwise, it saves the tag as ordinary HTML and passes it through unchanged.

- Program code in the server controls runs in response to various events, such as *OnLoad* and events from form fields. This program code can access server-side resources and change the properties of server controls as necessary.

- When all server control event handlers have finished, ASP.NET asks each control to render itself and sends the results, in sequence, to the Web visitor.

  - Conventional HTML tags go to the visitor unchanged.

  - In the case of server controls, ASP.NET doesn't send the XML that loaded the control. Instead, the control's *Render* method generates the HTML or other data that the visitor will receive.

- Once ASP.NET has sent the entire page to the visitor, it relinquishes all the objects that represented the page.

Categorizing ASP.NET Server Controls

As with almost everything in life, there are several way to categorize ASP.NET server controls. Technologically, the categories are:

- **Web Custom Controls** reside entirely within a DLL. Several projects or Web sites can therefore use a single copy of the control. This provides great assurance that the same code is running in each of those projects. However, to change the control you have to locate the original program code, change it, recompile it, and then replace all copies of the resulting DLL.

- **Web User Controls** consist of an .ascx file (which contains a fragment of HTML) and either source code files or a DLL. Each project or Web site that uses a user control must have its own copy of these files. This makes user controls easier to develop and modify, but harder to keep in sync across multiple projects.

As a practical matter, if you're developing an ASP.NET server control for use in one project or Web site, it's probably best to develop a user control. If you're developing a control for ongoing use in several projects or for sale as a product, a custom control is probably the better choice.

ASP.NET provides a rich selection of server controls. They're all Web custom controls, and they fall within two additional categories:

- **HTML Server Controls** duplicate the syntax and function of traditional HTML tags. Anytime you start with a traditional HTML tag and add *runat="server"*, you're creating an HTML server control.

New ASP.NET developers usually appreciate these controls because of their familiar syntax and because general-purpose Web design programs like Microsoft FrontPage® can display them accurately in graphical editing mode.

- **Web Server Controls** are more powerful than HTML server controls, but use a completely different syntax.

Do You Customize a User Control or Use a Custom Control?

Many new developers have trouble remembering the terms Web custom control and Web user control. To clarify the distinction, remember that:

- Web custom controls address the needs of many users and reside in a single DLL.
- Web user controls are easier for individual Web developers (users) to create and modify.

SEE ALSO

Chapter 8 will explain how to create and use your own Web user controls.

The following code, for example, creates an *HtmlSelect* control that displays a drop-down list of continents.

```
<select id="selContinent" runat="server">

    <option value="AF">Africa</option>

    <option value="AS">Asia</option>

    <option value="AU">Australia</option>

    <option value="EU">Europe</option>

    <option value="NA">North America</option>

    <option value="SA">South America</option>

</select>
```

The next block of code creates a *DropDownList* Web server control that renders an identical drop-down list.

```
<asp:DropDownList id="ddlContinent" runat="server">

    <asp:ListItem Value="AF">Africa</asp:ListItem>

    <asp:ListItem Value="AS">Asia</asp:ListItem>

    <asp:ListItem Value="AU">Australia</asp:ListItem>

    <asp:ListItem Value="EU">Europe</asp:ListItem>

    <asp:ListItem Value="NA">North America</asp:ListItem>

    <asp:ListItem Value="SA">South America</asp:ListItem>

</asp:DropDownList>
```

Why use the more complex and less familiar Web server control? One common reason is that only the DropDownList Web server control can generate events on the server. For example, if you add the attributes shown below in green to the preceding tag:

```
<asp:DropDownList id="ddlContinent" AutoPostBack="True"

OnSelectedIndexChanged="ddlContinent_SelectedIndexChanged"

runat="server">
```

- The *AutoPostBack="True"* attribute tells the control to generate JavaScript code that immediately submits the page to the Web server whenever the visitor selects a different continent.

- The *OnSelectedIndexChanged* attribute tells the control to run an event handler named *ddlContinent_SelectedIndexChanged* whenever the page goes out to the browser and comes back with a different continent selected.

That event handler might, for example, reload a second DropDownList server control with the names of countries in the given continent.

The most powerful Web server controls abandon all semblance of conventional HTML tags. They create clickable calendars, drop-down or fly-out menus, site maps, breadcrumbs, login buttons, self-registration forms, and a wide variety of additional useful prewritten objects. All of these, however, render themselves as ordinary HTML, and therefore work with any browser.

In Summary...

ASP.NET runs Web pages by loading them into memory as a collection of ordinary HTML segments and server controls. It then fires events at each server control, causing designated functions or subroutines (event handlers) to run. Finally, ASP.NET gets the visitor's HTML by calling each control's *Render* method.

There are two main types of server control. Web user controls are easier to develop, but Web custom controls are better for widespread deployment.

ASP.NET comes with two kinds of built-in server controls. HTML server controls resemble conventional HTML tags in form and function. Web server controls require tags with little resemblance to ordinary HTML, but they provide many specialized features and they do send ordinary HTML to the browser. Technologically, both HTML server controls and Web server controls are Web custom controls.

The next chapter will explain how to work with any program code that your ASP.NET page requires.

TIP
Chapter 8 will explain how to add and configure both HTML server controls and Web server controls on any ASP.NET page.

Chapter 3
Creating a New Web Site

In Microsoft® Visual Web Developer™, as in general practice, a Web site is a set of Web pages and associated files that you intend to create, deploy, and manage as a unit.

If you like, you can choose to treat an entire virtual Web server or domain name as one Web site. Frequently, however, you'll have sections of content that you want to create at different times, deploy at different times, control with different security, or otherwise manage separately. Fortunately, with ASP.NET 2.0, you can begin a new site at any folder in your server's content tree (that is, in its URL space.)

> **TIP**
> There's no firm rule governing the size of an ASP.NET 2.0 Web site. Most sites, however, have between several dozen and several hundred Web pages.

Choosing Where to Put the Working Copy of Your Site

Aligning Visual Web Developer Sites and IIS Applications

Even if you develop and test your Web site on the Development Server built into Visual Web Developer, you'll eventually need to run it on a full copy of IIS. There are two reasons for this:

- *The development server is only accessible from your own computer.*
- *IIS is the only full-access Web server that supports ASP.NET 2.0.*

Unfortunately, IIS doesn't divide a Web server into sites the same way that Visual Web Developer does. Instead, IIS divides Web servers into applications. In essence:

- *A site is a folder tree that Visual Web Developer manages as a unit.*
- *An application is a folder tree that IIS manages as a unit.*

Continued on next page

Most ASP.NET developers keep at least two copies of each site they develop: a working copy and a production copy.

- The working copy usually resides in an off-line or private area, isolated from the site's intended audience. After all, the working copy is work-in-progress. It's probably incomplete and less than fully functional. There's a *reason* you're still working on it.

- The production copy, or "live" site, resides on a Web server accessible to the site's audience. When the working copy is finally, uh, working and approved, the developer or an administrator copies the working copy to the live site.

Because ASP.NET is a technology that runs program code on a Web server, you need a Web server to test an ASP.NET Web site. Furthermore, the Web server needs to be running ASP.NET 2.0. In general, this presents two choices:

- You can use Internet Information Server (IIS), Microsoft's premier Web server, installed either on your own computer or on a remote server.

- You can use the ASP.NET Development Server built into Visual Web Developer. This is a subset of IIS that Visual Web Developer starts on demand, and that runs until you quit Visual Web Developer.

Visual Web Developer supports interactive debugging of any program code you write. That means you can designate places where the code should stop and pause so you can inspect objects and variables, run the program one statement at a time, and so forth. However, when the debugger freezes your code, it also must freeze the entire Web server and this, of course, is upsetting to anyone else using the same server. To avoid such problems, most ASP.NET developers debug on their own computers, and not on a server they share with other people.

IMPORTANT

The ASP.NET Development Server works only locally. It can't serve pages to another computer. It's only suitable for testing pages on your own computer.

Creating an Empty Web Site

You can locate the working copy of an ASP.NET Web site in four kinds of places:

- A file system location, such as a folder on your computer's hard disk or a shared network folder.
- An IIS server running locally on your computer.
- An IIS server running remotely (that is, on another computer on your network).
- An IIS server with a file system accessible via FTP.

The following sections will describe these options in more detail and explain how to create a new Web site in each case.

Creating a File System Web Site

In a file system Web site, you can store the files for your Web site in any file system folder you like. This can be on your local computer or in a network file sharing location. Table 3-1 summarizes the advantages and drawbacks of this approach.

Advantages	Drawbacks
You don't need to have a full copy of IIS running on your computer. Instead, you can test pages by using the ASP.NET Development Server.	You can't test certain advanced features of IIS—such as HTTP-based authentication, application pooling, and ISAPI filters—on the ASP.NET Development Server.
You don't need administrative rights to create or debug local Web sites.	Co-workers can't preview the site directly from your computer. To permit previewing, you'd have to publish the site to a server running IIS.
The ASP.NET development server is only accessible from the local computer. This may reduce security vulnerabilities.	

Table 3-1
Advantages and Drawbacks of a File System Web Site

Continued from page 24

It's important that these two folder trees begin at the same folder. Otherwise, your Visual Web Developer site won't run properly on IIS. There are three way of flagging your site's root folder as an IIS application:

- *If you publish the site by using the Microsoft FrontPage® Server Extensions, the server extensions will flag the site's root folder as an IIS application.*
- *In the Microsoft IIS Manager administrative tool right-click the site's starting folder, choose Properties, and then on the Directory tab, under Application Settings, click the Create button. If you don't have permission to do this yourself, contact the server's support staff.*
- *Later in this chapter, a section titled Creating a Local IIS Web Site explains how to flag folders as IIS applications without leaving Visual Web Developer. However, this requires the same permissions as using IIS Manager.*

TO CREATE A FILE SYSTEM WEB SITE IN VISUAL WEB DEVELOPER

1 Choose **New Web Site** from the File menu.

2 When the New Web Site dialog box shown in Figure 3-1 appears, select a template in the Templates box. For example, choose ASP.NET Web Site.

3 In the Location field:

■ Select **File System** in the drop-down list box.

■ Type, select, or browse to the file system location you want.

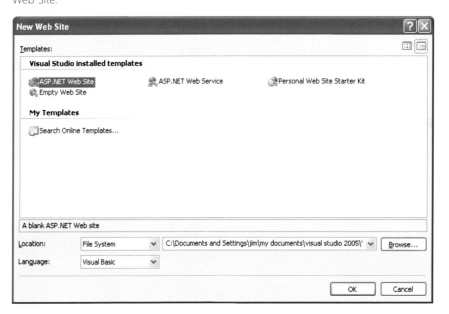

Figure 3-1
This dialog box is the launch point for creating a new Web site in Visual Web Developer.

4 In the Language drop-down list box, select the Web site's default programming language.

5 Click **OK**. Visual Web Developer creates the site, opens a default page in the page designer, and displays the folder in Solution Explorer.

If the path you specified already contains files, Visual Web Developer prompts you to specify a different folder name, open the existing Web site, or create the Web site anyway. In the last case, files from the template you select will overwrite any like-named files that already exist.

Creating a Local IIS Web Site

Local IIS Web sites run using a copy of IIS installed on your computer. Each Web site runs as its own IIS application. Visual Web Developer updates files by using the FrontPage server extensions or by accessing the file system directly. Table 3-2 summarizes the advantages and drawbacks of this approach.

Advantage	Drawbacks
You can test all IIS features including HTTP-based authentication, application pooling, and ISAPI filters. The site is accessible from other computers. (However, it's your responsibility to ensure that only the people you want have access.)	You must have administrative rights to create or debug IIS Web sites. Only one user on the computer can debug IIS at a time. Local IIS Web sites have remote access enabled by default. This may not be appropriate in some situations.

Table 3-2
Advantages and Drawbacks of a Local IIS Web Site

To create a local IIS Web site, you must first satisfy these requirements:

- You must be logged onto your computer with administrator privileges. Only an administrator can modify the necessary IIS settings.
- IIS must be installed on your computer and must be running.
- ASP.NET 2.0 must be installed on the computer and enabled in IIS.

The files in a local IIS Web site can reside anywhere you like. Here are some examples:

- You can create a new site under the IIS root (typically C:\InetPub\wwwroot) and mark it as an IIS application.
- You can create a new site at any folder location on your computer, then tell Visual Web Developer to mark it as both an IIS virtual directory and an IIS application.
- You can create a Web site that points to an existing IIS application, and then edit the files in that application.

TO CREATE A LOCAL IIS WEB SITE

1 Choose **New Web Site** from the File menu.

2 When the New Web Site dialog box appears, select any template listed in the Templates box.

3 Select HTTP in the Location drop-down list box.

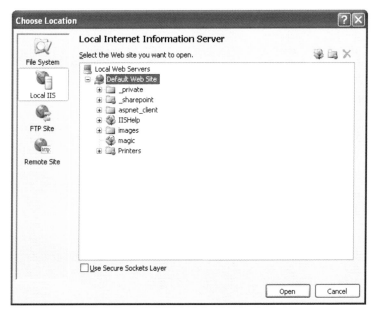

4 .If you want to hand-type the new site's URL, locate it's files in the Web Server's usual content space (for example, within C:\InetPub\wwwroot), and make the site an IIS application, proceed as follows:

■ Type the new URL into the Location Text box. For example, type *http://localhost/ContosoMagic.*

■ Skip to step 9.

Otherwise, take these steps:

■ Click the Browse button. This displays the Choose Location dialog box shown in Figure 3-2.

■ Click the Local IIS icon to display the list of local Web servers.

Figure 3-2
This dialog box displays a list of local Web servers and their URL spaces. Use it to select the parent folder of the new Web site you want to create.

5 If you want the new Web site to use files from an existing IIS application, select the folder where the existing application begins, click the Open button, and then skip to step 9.

6 In the box titled Select The Web Site Your Want To Open, select the Web server and then, if necessary, the parent folder of the site you want to create. For example, if you want to create a site at /doves/ white, select /doves.

7 If you want the new Web site's files to reside within the Web server's usual content space, use the Choose Location dialog box as follows:

■ Click the Create New Web Application button. This is the first of three buttons that appear near the top right corner of the dialog box.

■ A new folder named WebSite will appear in the Select The Web Site You Want To Open box. Rename this folder to the name you want.

If you want the new Web site's files to reside elsewhere, take these steps:

■ Click the Create New Virtual Directory button. This is the middle button that appears near the top right corner of the Choose Location dialog box. Clicking it displays the New Virtual Directory dialog box shown in Figure 3-3.

■ In the Alias Name box, type the URL path where you want the new site to reside.

■ In the Folder box, type or browse to the physical location where the Web site files will reside.

■ Click OK to create the virtual directory.

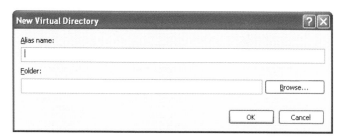

Figure 3-3
This dialog box defines a folder in the Web server's URL space and associates it with a physical file location.

8 Click the **Open** button to create the site in IIS.

9 Select the Web site's default programming language.

10 Click **OK** to create the site and open it in Visual Web Developer.

If the path you specified already contains files, Visual Web Developer will display a warning prompt.

Creating a Remote IIS Web Site

A remote Web site uses a copy of IIS installed on another computer that you can access over a network. Your Web site files reside on the remote computer and Visual Web Developer communicates with the Web site via the FrontPage Server Extensions. Table 3-3 presents the advantages and disadvantages of this approach.

To create a remote IIS Web site requires the following:

■ The remote computer must be running the 2.0 version of the .NET Framework.

■ The remote computer must have IIS installed and running.

- ASP.NET must be enabled in IIS on the remote computer.

- The FrontPage Server Extensions must be installed and enabled at the root level where you're creating the site.

- You must have FrontPage administration or author permissions to create new folders and files on the remote computer.

Advantage	Drawbacks
You can test the Web site in the same environment as the production server (or, if you feel lucky, directly on the production server). Multiple developers can work on the same site at the same time	Configuring the shared server for debugging can be complex. Only one developer can debug the application at a time. In addition, the server suspends all other requests while the developer is stepping through code.

Table 3–3
Advantages and Drawbacks of a Remote IIS Web Site

TO CREATE A REMOTE IIS WEB SITE

1 Choose **New Web Site** from the File menu.

2 When the New Web Site dialog box appears, select a template that appears in the Templates box.

3 In the Location field, select **HTTP** in the drop-down list box.

4 At your discretion. follow one of these procedures.

- Type the new site's URL into the Location box. For example, type *http://www.example.com/ ContosoMagic*

- Click the **Browse** button, select **Remote Site**, then type the URL you want into the Web Site Location box.

■ Click the **Browse** button, select **Remote Site**, click the **New Web Site** button, and then type the URL you want into the Web URL box.

5 Select the Web site's default programming language.

6 Click **OK** to create the site and open it in Visual Web Developer.

Visual Web Developer creates the site, opens a default page in the page designer, and displays the folder in Solution Explorer. If the path you specified already contains files, Visual Web Developer prompts you to specify a different location.

Creating an FTP-Accessible Web Site

On some Web servers, the only way to update files is by using File Transfer Protocol (FTP). This is often the case on servers provided by commercial hosting services. Visual Web Developer supports this environment. Specifically:

■ Whenever Visual Web Developer needs to read or write a file, it does so via FTP.

■ If the FTP location is also within the content tree of an IIS Web server running ASP.NET 2.0, you can run and test your site from the same server.

Table 3-4 summarizes the advantages and drawbacks of an FTP-accessible Web site.

Advantage	Drawbacks
You can directly open, test, and modify your site on the production Web server	You can't create an IIS application by FTP. If you work only on the FTP server, you have no backup copies of the site. Unless you take other precautions, the FTP copy is the only copy. Best practice is to test your site before it goes into production, and then publish the tested site by FTP.

Table 3-4
Advantages and Drawbacks of an
FTP-Accessible Web Site

To use this approach, the site you want to open must be available on an FTP server and you must get the following information from the FTP server administrator.

- The name of the FTP server where you want to open the Web site.
- The name of the FTP folder where you have permission to create and write files.

You might also need:

- A user name and password for the server.
- The port number that the FTP server uses. This is typically port 21.

TO CREATE AN FTP-ACCESSIBLE WEB SITE

1 Choose **New Web Site** from the File menu.

2 When the New Web Site dialog box appears, select a template from the Templates box.

3 In the Location field, select **FTP** in the drop-down list box.

4 If you wish, type or select the site's FTP location (such as http://ftp.example.com/public_html/ ContosoMagic). Otherwise, click the **Browse** button and make sure the FTP Site icon is selected. The Choose Location dialog box will resemble Figure 3-4.

5 Fill in the following fields, then click **Open**.

- **Server** Enter the name of the server, such as *ftp://ftp.example.com*.
- **Port** If the FTP server operates on a port other than 21, change this value.
- **Directory** Type the name of the FTP folder where you want the Web site files to reside. (This often differs from the HTTP folder, and from the physical file system folder as well.) For example, all the following might point to the same physical file location:

  FTP folder name: *public_html/ContosoMagic/*

  HTTP folder name ContosoMagic/

  File system folder name *C:\InetPub\wwwroot\ContosoMagic*

- **Passive Mode** Select this box if you have trouble communicating with the FTP server because of a firewall.

> **IMPORTANT**
>
> When Visual Web Developer creates a Web site via FTP, it can't perform the necessary step of configuring the Web site as an IIS application. Instead, you or a server administrator must use the IIS Manager administrative tool to configure the application.

■ **Anonymous Login** Select this box if the FTP server permits reading and writing files without logging in. Clear it if you need to enter a user name and password.

■ **User Name and Password** Enter credentials that provide the necessary access to your FTP file area. These might differ from your usual Microsoft Windows® login credentials.

6 Select the Web site's default programming language.

7 Click **OK** to create the site and open it in Visual Web Developer.

Visual Web Developer connects to the FTP server and copies the template files to that location. Don't forget that for new sites, you or a server administrator need to run the IIS Manager administrative tool and mark the site as an application.

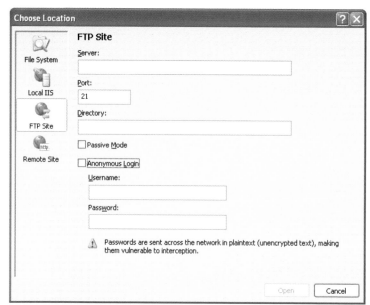

Figure 3-4
When connecting to an FTP site, the Choose Location dialog box provides these options

In Summary...

It's good practice to have at least two copies of any Web site you maintain: a development or "working" copy and a production or "live" version. Visual Web Developer can maintain working copies in four kinds of places: in a file system location, on a local IIS server, on a remote IIS server, or on an FTP-accessible server. The live site will usually reside on a remote IIS server

The next chapter will explain how to open existing sites.

Chapter 4

Opening an Existing Web Site

Web sites are decidedly high-maintenance. You create them once and then you maintain them forever. As a result, you'll probably open existing sites much more often than you create new ones. Fortunately, Microsoft® Visual Web Developer™ makes opening sites of either type very easy. This chapter explains the procedures you need to follow.

Opening a Recently-Used Web Site

When Visual Web Developer starts up, it displays the Start Page shown previously in Figure 1-2. On the Start Page, the Recent Projects box contains a clickable list of Web sites you recently opened. To open one of these sites again, simply click on it. When the Solution Explorer window shows an expandable list of the files and folders in the site, the site is open.

The same list of recent sites appears on the File menu. To open a site that way, choose Recent Projects from the File menu, then click on the site you want from the resulting submenu.

By default, Visual Web Developer remembers the last 10 sites you open. If you want it to remember more or fewer sites, proceed as follows.

TO REMEMBER MORE OR FEWER SITES

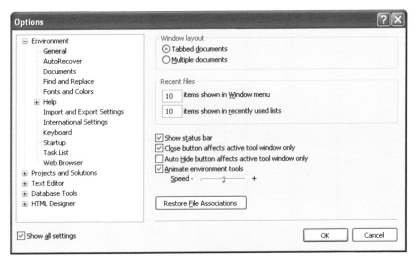

1 Choose **Options** from the Tools menu.

2 When the Options dialog box appears, locate the Show All Settings check box in the bottom left corner and make sure it's selected.

3 In the tree view at the left of the dialog box, open the Environment node and select **General**. The dialog box will then resemble Figure 4-1.

4 In the Recent Files area, locate the text box titled **Items Shown In Recently Used Lists** and type the number of sites you want Visual Web Developer to remember.

5 Click **OK**.

Figure 4-1
Visual Web Developer provides a myriad of configuration options. The second text box controls the length of recently used lists.

NOTE

In Figure 4-1, the text box titled Items Shown In Windows Menu specifies the maximum number of window names that Visual Web Developer will display after you click Window on the main menu.

Opening an Arbitrary Web Site

To open any existing Web site, regardless of whether you opened it recently or not, proceed as follows.

TO OPEN AN ARBITRARY WEB SITE

1 Choose **Open Web Site** from the File menu.

2 When the Open Web Site dialog box shown in Figure 4-2 appears, click the icon in the Places bar (on the left) that best describes your site's location.

3 Continue as directed in the next four sections. There's one section for each choice in the Places bar.

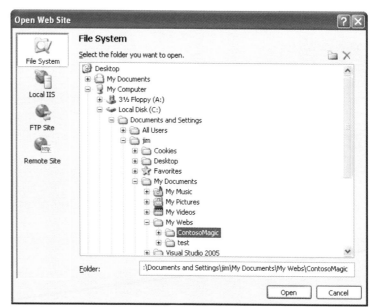

Figure 4-2
This version of the Open Web Site dialog box lets you select a site accessible via the Microsoft Windows® file system.

Opening a File System Web Site

After you click the File System icon in the Open Web Site dialog box, the display should resemble that shown in Figure 4-2.

TO OPEN A FILE SYSTEM WEB SITE

1 In the Open Web Site dialog box, open or close any necessary tree nodes, then locate and select the folder that contains the root of your Web site.

2 Click the **Open** button.

There's just one precaution: *Don't* use the Open Web Site command to open a folder that isn't the root of a Web site. This usually happens when you have a complex folder tree and:

- Some folders within that tree are Web site root folders.

- Some folders are just subfolders within a site.

When you use the Open Web Site command to open a folder, Visual Web Developer assumes that folder will be the root of a Web site, and that it'll be an IIS application, and that it's OK to store specially-named ASP.NET configuration files and subfolders there. If those assumptions aren't true, the site won't work as you expect. So again, whenever you use the Open Web Site command, make sure you're opening a Web site's root folder.

Opening a Local IIS Web Site

If you click the Local IIS icon in the Open Web Site dialog box, the display will change to the form shown in Figure 4-3.

This is essentially the same view of the Web server's URL space that the IIS Manager administrative tool displays.

> **NOTE**
>
> Two of the files that must reside in the root of an ASP.NET Web site are web.config and web.sitemap. The special subfolders bin, App_Code, App_Data, App_GlobalResources, App_LocalResources, App_WebReferences, App_Browsers, and App_Themes must also reside in the site's root folder.

TO OPEN A LOCAL IIS WEB SITE

1 Locate the folder that contains the root of your Web site. To do this, open or close any tree nodes as necessary.

2 Select the folder and click the **Open** button.

Notice that in Figure 4-3, two of the folder icons (*IISHelp* and *magic*) depict an open carton with a globe and a document inside. If a folder has this icon, it's the root of an IIS application. These root folders are the ones you should open in Visual Web Developer.

If you try to open a folder that's not the root of an IIS application, Visual Web Developer will display a warning message and ask if you want to continue. In almost every case, the correct answer is No. Then, to recover:

- If the folder you tried to open is part of another application, open that application.

- If the folder you tried to open *should* be the root of an IIS application, select it and click the Create New Web Application button (the leftmost of three in the top right corner of the dialog box).

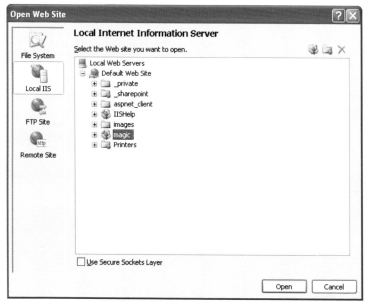

Figure 4-3
When you open a local IIS Web site, the Open Web Site dialog box displays this view of the Web server's URL space.

Opening an FTP-Accessible Web Site

If you click the FTP Site icon in the Open Web Site dialog box, the display will change to the form shown previously in Figure 3-4.

TO OPEN A WEB SITE ACCESSIBLE ONLY BY FTP

1 Fill out the fields as the section titled "Creating an FTP-Accessible Web Site" in Chapter 3 instructed you.

2 Click the **Open** button.

As when creating an FTP-accessible Web site, it's your job to ensure that the FTP location you specify corresponds to the root of an IIS application on the Web server.

Opening a Remote Web Site

If you click the Remote Site icon in the Open Web Site dialog box, the display will change to resemble Figure 4-4.

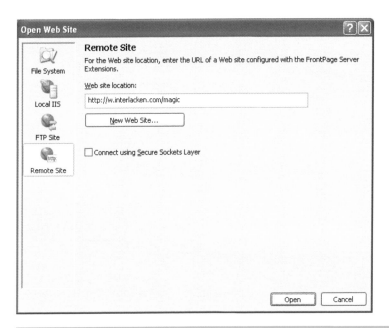

Figure 4-4
When you open a remote Web site,
there's no browse list to help you find
the correct Web server and path.

TO OPEN THE REMOTE WEB SITE

1 Type the Web site's full URL in the Web Site Location box. Alternatively, click the New Web Site button and create a site as the section titled "Creating a Remote IIS Web Site" in Chapter 3 instructed.

2 Click the **Open** button.

When opening a remote Web site in Visual Web Developer, you should be aware of these precautions:

- The site will only be accessible if the Microsoft FrontPage® Server Extensions are installed on the Web server. Visual Web Developer uses the FrontPage Server Extensions to read and write files on the server, to modify Web server settings, and to otherwise interact with the Web server..

- The folder you specify should be the root of a FrontPage Web site and the root of an IIS application. This will normally be the case for any Web sites you create in Visual Web Developer or in a full version of Microsoft Visual Studio®.

  If, for some reason, the location isn't the root of a FrontPage Web site, and you *did* specify the correct folder, convert the folder into a FrontPage server-based Web site using either the Microsoft FrontPage Server Extension Administration Web pages on the Web server or Microsoft FrontPage.

  If you specify the correct location and find it isn't the root of an IIS application, use the Microsoft IIS Manager administrative tool to mark the folder as an application, then try opening it again.

- The IIS application should be configured to use ASP.NET 2.0. If it isn't, Visual Web Developer displays a warning message and asks if you want to proceed. In almost every case, you should:

  1. Answer No to the prompt.

  2. Make sure version 2.0 of the .NET Framework is installed on the remote computer.

  3. Make sure the IIS application is configured to use ASP.NET 2.0.

  4. Try again to open the application in Visual Web Developer.

IIS can run any combination of ASP.NET 1.0, 1.1, and 2.0 applications on the same virtual Web server.

TO CHECK OR CONFIGURE THE VERSION OF ASP.NET FOR AN APPLICATION

1 Start the IIS Manager administrative tool.

2 In the left pane of the IIS Manager application, open:

■ The node for Internet Information Services.

■ The node for the computer in question.

■ The Web Sites node.

■ The node for the virtual server in question (i.e. Default Web Site).

■ The node for any parent folders you need to open so your IIS application's root folder is visible.

3 Right-click your application's root folder, then choose **Properties** from the resulting shortcut menu.

4 When the application's Properties dialog box appears, click the **ASP.NET** tab. The dialog box should then resemble Figure 4-5.

5 Set the ASP.NET version drop-down list to the most recent version of ASP.NET 2.0 installed on the server, then click the **OK** button.

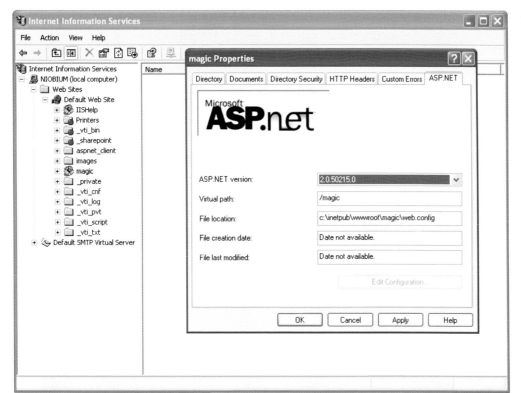

Figure 4-5
This dialog box from IIS Manager configures the version of ASP.NET that an IIS application will use.

In Summary...

Visual Web Developer provides several different ways of opening an existing Web site. Two of these are the Recent Projects list and the Open Web Site command on the File menu. Using these commands, Visual Web Developer can open Web sites that reside at a file system path, on a local IIS server, on a remote server accessible by FTP, or on a remote server running the FrontPage server extensions..

The next chapter will explain how to copy a site from place to place (for example, from a live production site to a work area, or vice versa).

Chapter 5

Copying Your Web Site

Any time you have multiple copies of a Web site—such as a working copy and a live production copy—it's certain that from time to time you'll need to copy one or more files from one location to another, or even copy the entire site! For example, you may wish to start a new working copy based on your live site, or you might need to copy completed changes from the working copy to the production site.

Microsoft® Visual Web Developer™ has built-in features that make this easy, and this chapter explains how those features work.

Specifying the Source and Remote Web Sites

TO COPY A SITE FROM ONE LOCATION TO ANOTHER

1 Start Visual Web Developer.

2 Open one site as directed in Chapter 4.

3 Choose **Copy Web Site** from the Website menu. This displays the Copy Web window shown in Figure 5-1.

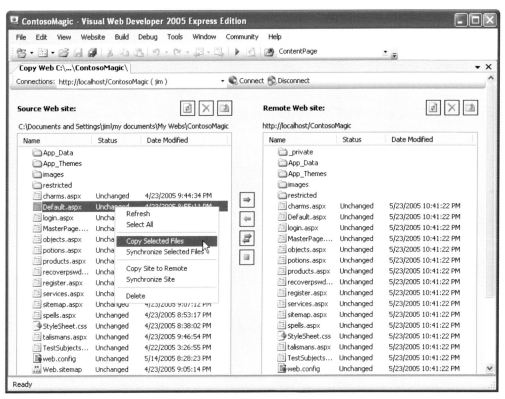

■ **Source Web Site** This area occupies the left side of the window. It shows the contents of the site you opened in step 1.

■ **Remote Web Site** This area occupies the right side of the window. Initially, it may be blank. In general, though, it shows the contents of the other site involved in the copy operation. By default, this is the remote Web site you opened most recently.

Despite these areas being named Source and Remote, neither distance nor direction make any difference. For example:

■ The source site could be half way around the world and the remote site could be on your own computer.

■ You can copy files from remote to local as easily as from local to remote.

If the Source and Remote areas display the correct pair of Web sites, skip to the next section in this chapter. Otherwise, continue to step 4.

Figure 5-1
The Copy Web feature displays the contents of two Web sites and copies any files you like between them.

4 Open the **Connections** drop-down list in the top left corner of the Copy Web window. If the remote Web site you want appears in this list, select it and Visual Web Developer will display that site in the Remote Web Site portion of the window. Once this occurs, skip to the next section in this chapter.

5 Click the **Connect** button near the top center of the Copy Web window. This displays the Open Web Site dialog box shown previously in Figures 4-2, 4-3, and 4-4.

6 Use the Open Web Site dialog box just as Chapter 4 instructed. Keep in mind, however, that you're opening the remote Web site for a Copy Web operation. The source Web site you opened in step 1 will still appear on the left.

Selecting and Copying Files

The Source Web Site and Remote Web Site portions of the Copy Web dialog box each display the contents of one folder from their respective sites.

- To view the contents of a subfolder, double-click it.
- To view the contents of a parent folder, click the Navigate Up One Directory Level button just above the top right corner of the listing.

If you right-click either folder listing, a shortcut menu will offer the following commands:

- **Refresh** Reloads the file and folder listing. Use this command if you suspect updates from another source have superseded the information on display. The Refresh buttons just above the top right corner of each folder listing perform the same function.
- **Select All** Selects all the files and folders in the folder listing you right-clicked.
- **Copy Selected Files** Copies all currently-selected files and folders from the listing you right-clicked to the other location.

> **TIP**
> To select multiple files in either the source or remote Web site, use Shift+click or Ctrl+click just as you would in Microsoft Windows® Explorer. Selecting a folder selects all its files and subfolders.

- **Synchronize Selected Files** Copies selected files from either site that are absent or older on the other site. At completion, the same files and folders—with all the newest time stamps—will exist on both sites.

- **Copy Site To Remote (or Source)** Copies the entire source Web site to the remote Web site, or vice versa. The single-arrow buttons between the two folder listings also perform these functions.

- **Synchronize Site** Works like Synchronize Selected Files, except that it pertains to the entire Web site. The double-arrow button between the two folder listings also performs this function.

- **Delete** Deletes the selected files. The Delete buttons just above the top right corner of each folder listing perform the same function.

The square button between the two folder listings provides a Cancel function. If a copy operation seems to be running too slowly, or if it might be hung, click this button to terminate the process.

Keep in mind that when copying files between two existing sites, some files *ought* to be different. For example:

- When you copy a working copy of your site to the live production version, you probably *don't* want to overwrite your production databases. Frequently, these reside in your site's *App_Data* folder.

- The *web.config* file contains a myriad of settings that affect your site. Many of these settings might be the same for development and testing, but many may be different as well. For example, this is where Visual Web Developer stores the name, location, userid, and password for accessing your database. These settings are usually different for testing than they are for production.

IMPORTANT
Think carefully before copying the *App_Data* folder from one site to another. *Don't* overwrite your production databases!

IMPORTANT
Think carefully before copying the *web.config* file from one site to another. *Don't* overwrite the run-time settings for your production site!

Finally, keep in mind that Visual Web Developer supports several different ways of compiling any program code your site contains.

- In some approaches, the Web server compiles the code for each page at run-time; that is, the first time a visitor requests that page. In these situations, you need to copy all your source code to the production site.

- In other cases, you compile the code before you copy the site. In this environment, you need to copy the compilation output (a DLL) but not the source code.

   Chapter 7 will explain more about these options.

MORE INFO

For more information about compiling program code and deciding which files need to be on your live production site, refer to, "Storing, Compiling, and Publishing Program Code," in Chapter 7.

In Summary...

Visual Web Developer provides a Copy Web command that can copy all or part of one Web site to another. This is very useful for creating a new working copy of your production site, and for copying completed changes from the working copy to the production site.

The next chapter will explain how to create and modify the Web pages in your site.

Chapter 6

Creating and Modifying Web Pages

Once you have a Web site, or at least a working copy of one, you'll certainly want to create and modify the Web pages it contains. Creating pages is far more work—yet far more interesting—than creating a blank site. This chapter explains how to create pages in Microsoft® Visual Web Developer™, how to open existing pages, and how to add and modify page content.

In reading this material, keep in mind that a *control* means any ordinary HTML tag or ASP.NET server control. In this sense, tags like <br>, <img src="logo.gif">, <form runat="server">, complex server controls, and even the Web page itself are all controls.

TO CREATE OR OPEN A WEB PAGE

It's easy to create a new Web page in Visual Web Developer. Simply follow this procedure:

1 Open the site that will contain the page.

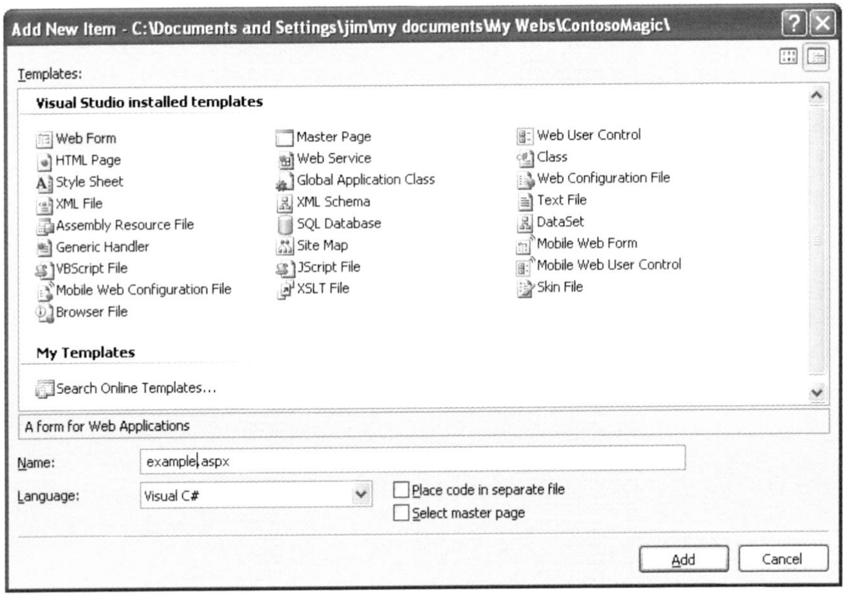

Figure 6-1
When you create a new file for your site, this dialog box prompts for the type of file you want.

2 Choose New File from the File menu. This displays the Add New Item page shown in Figure 6-1.

Here's how to complete the entries on the Add New Item page:

■ **Template** If your page will use any ASP.NET features, select Web Form. This is almost always the correct choice.

If you choose HTML Page, Visual Web Developer will assign an .htm filename extension. This, in turn, bypasses all ASP.NET processing when the Web server delivers the page to visitors.

For a brief description of the other templates, temporarily select each one and read the description that appears in the untitled gray box below the selection area. Later chapters will explain what to do with many of these templates.

■ **Name** Specify a filename for the new page. For Web Forms, the default and required extension is .aspx.

MORE INFO

For more information about organizing ASP.NET program code, refer to the section titled, "Storing, Compiling, and Publishing Program Code," in Chapter 7.

■ **Language** Specify the programming language you want to use for ASP.NET program code (that is, for program code that runs on the Web server). In Visual Web Developer Express, the choices are Microsoft Visual Basic®, C#, and J#.

■ **Place Code In Separate File** Select this box if you want the Web page's HTML code and its ASP.NET program code to reside in separate files. Clear it to keep both kinds of code in the same file.

- **Select Master Page** Select this box if you want the new page to inherit the appearance of a special template you've created for your site. After you click the Add button, Visual Web Developer will then display a Select A Master Page dialog box where you specify the master page you want.

MORE INFO

For more information about ASP.NET Master Pages, refer to Chapter 9, "Using Master Pages to Centralize Page Layout."

There are many ways of opening an existing page in Visual Web Developer. Here are three of the most common:

- Double-click a file name in the Solution Explorer window.

- Choose Open File from the File menu. This displays a standard File Open dialog box where you can choose the file you want.

- Choose Recent Files from the File menu and then select a file from the resulting submenu.

Working with Web Page Views

For each Web page you open, Visual Web Developer provides a choice of two distinct editing modes. These are:

- **Design View** Provides an editable, visual preview of the Web page. However, keep these exceptions in mind:

  - Design view doesn't actually run any program code or server controls your page might contain. Instead it displays simulated results, blank form fields, and other placeholders.

  - Design view may display controls that run on the Web server but display nothing in the browser. Typically, such controls provide background functions such as connecting to databases. This is so you know the controls exist and so you can select them for editing.

  - Design view doesn't react to mouse clicks, key presses, and other events as a browser would. Instead, these events (and others) invoke features that are part of Visual Web Developer. Clicking a hyperlink, for example, doesn't display the target page in Design View. Instead, it selects the hyperlink for editing.

- **Source View** Displays the source code for your page. In addition to HTML code, this includes types such as:

  - CSS (Cascading Style Sheet) code unique to your page.

  - XML tags that load ASP.NET server controls.

  - JavaScript code that runs on the browser.

  - Visual Basic, C#, or J# code that runs on the Web server.

To switch between Design view and Source view, click the Design or Source tab at the bottom of the editing window.

The remainder of this chapter deals exclusively with Design view editing. The next chapter, "Working with Source Code," will explain Source view editing.

Adding Controls

Once you have a blank page, your next task will be adding text, pictures, form fields, or other controls the page requires. This section explains, in a general way, how to perform these tasks.

Adding Controls from the Toolbox

When your page needs to use one of the server controls that comes with Visual Web Developer, you should immediately think of using the Toolbox window. This window is also useful for adding standard HTML controls to your page. It appears along the left edge of Figure 6-2.

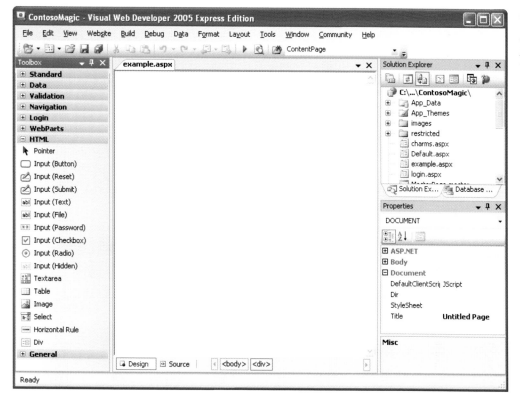

Figure 6-2
The Toolbox at the left of this display contains a rich assortment of controls you can add to your Web pages. To see the individual controls in a group, click that group's plus sign (+).

Visual Web Developer organizes Toolbox controls into functional groups, then it displays or hides each group depending on the type of file you're editing. Table 6-1, for example, lists the toolbox groups that appear for an ASP.NET (.aspx) Web page. For ordinary (.htm) Web pages, only the HTML and General groups appear.

Table 6-1
Toolbox Groups for Web Forms

Group	Description
Standard	General-purpose Web server controls. Many of these are similar to HTML controls, but are more functional.
Data	Server controls designed for accessing, displaying, and updating database information.
Validation	Server controls that verify the syntax of data that visitors enter in form fields.
Navigation	Server controls that display breadcrumbs and drop-down, fly-out, and tree view menus.
Login	Server controls for developing self-registration and access control features.
WebParts	Server controls that treat portions of the Web page as dynamic areas that authorized visitors can customize to suit their personal preferences. Chapter 18, "Displaying and Customizing Web Parts," will explain this much further.
HTML	Ordinary HTML controls. After adding an ordinary HTML control to an ASP.NET (.aspx) page, you can convert it to an HTML server control.
General	Initially empty. Typically, this contains additional controls you purchase or develop yourself.

Visual Web Developer provides three different ways of adding Toolbox items to a page. They all produce the same results. Just choose the one you like the best:

- Set the insertion point where you want the control to appear, then double-click its Toolbox entry.

- Drag the control you want from the Toolbox window and drop it on an open Web page.

- In the Toolbox window, copy the control you want to the clipboard, then set the insertion point and paste the control onto your Web page.

When working with the Toolbox or with controls already on a page, any standard Cut, Copy, or Paste procedure will do. For example, to copy something to the clipboard, first select it then press Ctl+C, right-click and choose Copy, or choose Copy from the Edit menu.

Adding Tables and Layers from the Menu Bar

Although you can create an HTML table by using the Table entry in the Toolbox's HTML group, this method provides little flexibility. You get the same initial table properties every time. For more flexibility, try the following procedure.

TO ADD TABLES AND LAYERS FROM THE MENU BAR

1 Set the insertion point where you want the table to appear.

2 Choose **Insert Table** from the Layout menu.

3 Fill out the Insert Table dialog box, then click **OK**.

If you wish, you can also add layers to your page this way. Just set the insertion point and then choose Insert Layer from the Layout menu. However, Visual Web Developer won't display an Insert Layer dialog box. You get a generic layer, just as if you'd used the Div entry in the Toolbox's HTML group.

Adding Controls from Solution Explorer

If a file appears in Solution Explorer, you can generally add it to an open page by dragging and dropping. That is, you can drag the filename from Solution Explorer and drop it onto an open Web page. The results you get from this method depend on the type of file. Here are some examples:

- If you drag a picture file (for example, one with a .gif or .jpg filename extension), Visual Web Developer creates an <img> tag that displays that picture.

- If you drag a Cascading Style Sheet (.css) file, Visual Web Developer links that stylesheet to your page.

MORE INFO

For more information about ASP. NET User controls, refer to Chapter 8, "Creating and Using Web User Controls."

- If you drag a User control (that is, a file with an .ascx filename extension), Visual Web Developer adds:

  - A <% @Control . . . %> tag that points to the .ascx file and assigns it a tag name (unless such a tag already exists).

  - An XML tag with the given tag name. This loads the control in the location where you drop it.

- If you drag a Web page (for example, one with an .htm or .aspx filename extension) Visual Web Developer creates a link to that page. The filename will be the hyperlink text.

If dragging a file from Solution Explorer doesn't produce the results you want, simply press Ctrl+Z (undo) and use the Toolbox to create the type of control you want.

Setting Control Properties

Once you've added an HTML or server control to your page, you'll almost certainly want to modify one or more of its properties. This section describes the variety of ways you can modify such properties without leaving Design view.

Setting Properties with the Properties Window

Visual Web Developer provides a Properties window that displays and edits the properties of any control you choose. A version of this window appears in the bottom right corner of Figure 6-3.

TIP

Expect minor variations in the way the Properties window works for various controls.

The Properties window always displays the properties of the currently-selected control. To select a control and display its properties, right-click it and choose Properties. However, simply selecting the control usually has the same effect.

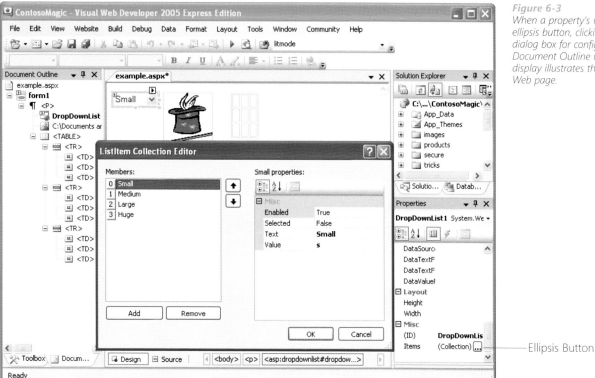

Figure 6-3
When a property's value box contains an ellipsis button, clicking that button displays a dialog box for configuring that property. The Document Outline window at the left of this display illustrates the structure of your Web page.

Ellipsis Button

If you have difficulty selecting the exact control you want, refer to the Quick Tag Toolbar at the bottom of the editing window. This is the toolbar that displays <body> <div> in Figure 6-2 and <body> <p> <asp:dropdownlist#dropdow . . . > in Figure 6-3.

The Quick Tag Toolbar always displays a tag name for the current control and all its containers, up to and including the <body> tag. For an HTML table cell, for example, the Quick Tag toolbar displays <body> <table> <tr> <td>. (If necessary, use the arrow buttons to scroll the list of tags left or right.) Clicking any of these tag names selects the corresponding control.

The Document Outline window that appears along the left edge of Figure 6-3 provides another way of locating and selecting the control you want.

- To display this window, choose Document Outline from the View menu.
- To select a control, select it in the Document Outline window. This selects the same control in Design view and displays its properties in the Properties window.

Once you've selected the control you want to modify, you're ready to start using the Properties window. The first control in the this window is a drop-down list that shows two types of items:

- All parents of the current control.
- All server controls in the current page.

To select and then modify the properties of any of these controls, select that control from the drop-down list.

The second control in the Properties window is a toolbar that displays up to five buttons. Some buttons may be absent or dimmed, depending on the control. These buttons are, in order:

- **Categorized** Groups the list of properties by category. Figure 6-3 shows this option in effect for a *DropDownList* control. This control has six categories: Accessibility, Appearance, Behavior, Data, Layout, and Misc. The categories for other controls will likely be different.

- **Alphabetical** Lists all properties in alphabetical order, with no category headings.

- **Properties** Specifies that you want the Properties window to display the control's properties as in Figure 6-3.

- **Events** Specifies that you want the Properties window to display the control's events.

  The Properties window only lists events that cause ASP.NET to run code on the Web server. It doesn't list events that code on the browser will handle.

- **Property Pages** Displays a specialized dialog box, if any, that configures the control's properties. Only a few controls have such dialog boxes.

To modify a property, click the value box at the right of the property title. Then, proceed as follows:

- If the value appears as text, type it or edit it.
- If a drop-down arrow appears at the right of the value box, click it and select a value from the resulting list.
- If an ellipsis (. . .) button appears as shown in Figure 6-3, click it and use the resulting dialog box to configure the property.

If you want to write code that runs on the Web server whenever a certain event occurs, take the following steps.

TO WRITE SERVER CODE THAT RESPONDS TO A WEB PAGE EVENT

1 Select the control that raises the event.

2 When the control's properties appear in the Properties window, click the Events button.

3 Double-click the event you want to act upon (i.e. *handle*). Visual Web Developer will switch to Source view and create a dummy (i.e. empty) event handler. Add the program code you want within this event handler.

4 After you return to Design view, the Properties window will display the new event handler's name after the event name.

5 To make the Properties window once again display the control's properties, click the Properties button.

Setting Properties with the Mouse

In Design view you can move and resize many Web page controls by using standard Windows mouse movements. For example:

- To resize a control, select it and then drag one edge or a sizing handle.

- To reposition a control, first select it, then move the mouse over its interior. When the mouse pointer takes on this appearance:

    drag the control to the new location you want.

    Some controls, like the *LoginView* control shown below, display a Move decoration whenever it's possible to relocate the control by dragging. In such cases, you can move the control by dragging the Move decoration.

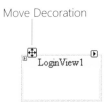

Move Decoration

- You can also move controls by cutting and pasting.
- To duplicate a control, copy and paste it.

    Don't overlook the commands that appear on shortcut menus when you right-click a control. For the most part these should be very familiar: Cut, Copy, Paste, Delete, and so forth. The following commands, however, are worth special mention:

- **Style** Displays a Style Builder dialog box where you can configure CSS properties for the control.

- **Run As Server Control** Converts an ordinary HTML control to an HTML server control. You need to do this if you want server-side code to manipulate the control or its contents.

- **Edit Image** Loads a picture into the editor your computer associates with the picture's file type.

- **Show Smart Tag** Displays a special *task menu* that displays commands and settings unique to a specific type of control. The next section explains smart tags and task menus.

- **Auto Format** Displays an Auto Format dialog box where you can choose to apply pre-made formatting schemes to the control.

- **Edit Template** Displays a submenu listing of all the templates applicable to the given control. Selecting a template displays a task menu with commands for modifying that template. One of these commands is End Template Editing , which saves changes and closes the task menu.

- **Refresh** Displays the current Web page from scratch. This corrects any flaws in the current display.

- **Properties** Selects the control and displays its properties in the Properties window. However, for a few controls, this command also displays a specialized dialog box for configuring the control.

Setting Properties with Smart Tags

Some types of controls have a special decoration called a smart tag. Clicking this decoration displays a task menu unique to that control. Figure 6-4 shows the smart tag and the resulting task menu for a *GridView* control. This type of control displays information from a *Data Source* (i.e. from a database).

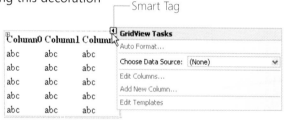

In this example, the Auto Format and Edit Template commands work as the previous section described for regular shortcut commands. The Choose Data Source, Edit Columns, and Add New Column commands are specific to the *GridView* control.

If you can't find the specialized property settings for a specific control, try looking for a smart tag and its resulting task menu.

Figure 6-4
Some controls have smart tags that display specialized task menus for that control.

Setting Properties with the Format Menu

Visual Web Developer has a Format menu that automates many common formatting tasks. For the most part, the commands on this menu work like those on the Format menu of any other Microsoft Windows® program.

Visual Web Developer also has a Layout menu that provides commands for adding and modifying HTML tables, for adding Layers (<div> tags), and for specifying CSS positioning properties for any control. The Layout menu appears in Figure 6-5.

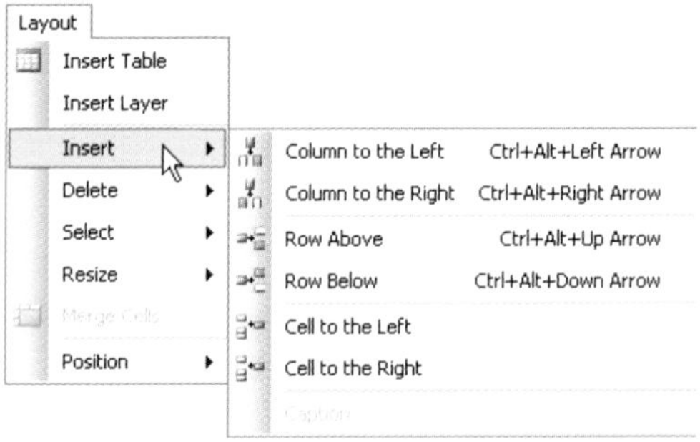

For the most part, these commands work very much as you'd expect. The Insert Table and Insert, Delete, Select, Resize, and Merge Cells commands only apply to HTML tables.

The Position command sets the current control's CSS positioning mode to Absolute, Relative, Static, or Not Set. These are standard CSS properties.

TIP

To set a control's *top, left, height,* and *width* properties, choose Style from the Format menu and then click Position.

Figure 6-5
The Layout menu provides a useful assortment of commands for working with HTML tables and layers.

Setting Properties with Toolbars

Visual Web Developer includes two toolbars that modify the appearance and position of controls. These are:

- **The Formatting Toolbar** is similar to those you find in Microsoft Office applications. First you select the text or control you want to modify, then you click the drop-down list or button for the property you want to set. Many commands on the Formatting toolbar duplicate those on the Format menu.

- **The Layout Toolbar** applies only to controls that use *absolute positioning*. This is a CSS technique that forces controls to appear at specific x-y coordinates on the Web page.

If you want to use absolute positioning for every control on your page, follow this procedure.

TO USE ABSOLUTE POSITIONING FOR EVERY CONTROL ON A PAGE

1 Choose **Position** from the Layout menu, and then choose **Auto-Position Options**.

2 When the Options dialog box shown in Figure 6-6 appears, make sure the HTML Designer tree node is open and CSS Positioning is selected.

3 To use absolute positioning for any controls you subsequently add to a page:

■ Select the check box titled Change Positioning To The Following For Controls Added Using The Toolbox, Paste, Or Drag And Drop.

■ Choose Absolutely Positioned from the drop-down list.

4 If you want Visual Web Developer to "snap" absolute positioning measurements to exact multiples of a pixel:

■ Select the check box titled Snap Pixel-based Positions And Sizes To The Following Setting.

■ Use the Horizontal Spacing and Vertical Spacing text boxes to a specify the grid size you want.

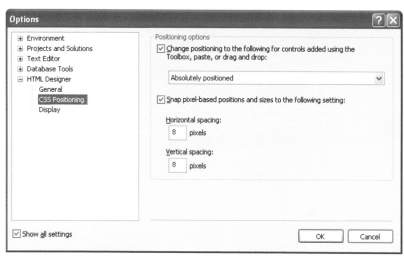

Figure 6-6
These settings in the Options dialog box control the use of absolute positioning for controls you subsequently add to a page.

Adding or Modifying Hyperlinks

Visual Web Developer can convert any picture or text on your page to a hyperlink. Here's the procedure.

TO ADD OR MODIFY A HYPERLINK

1 Select the text or picture you want to be a hyperlink.

2 Take any *one* of these actions:

■ Choose Convert To Hyperlink from the Format menu.

■ Click the Convert To Hyperlink button on the Formatting toolbar.

■ Press Ctrl+L.

3 When the Hyperlink dialog box appears, select the protocol (such as *http:*) and then either:

■ Click the Browse button to select a hyperlink destination from the current Web site

■ Key in the URL.

4 Click the **OK** button.

To specify additional hyperlink properties, select the hyperlink and use the Properties window, just as you would for any other control.

In Summary...

In Visual Web Developer, adding controls to a Web page is easy. Depending on the type of control, you can drag it from the Toolbox, drag it from Solution Explorer, or insert it using a menu.

Once the control is part of your page, you can modify it by selecting it and using the Properties window, by dragging or stretching it with the mouse, by right-clicking it and using a shortcut menu, by clicking its smart tag and using a task menu, by using main menu commands, by using the formatting or positioning toolbar.

Chapter 7 will explain the various ways that Visual Web Developer can work with source code.

Chapter 7

Working with Source Code

If you've never used an advanced programming editor to create Web pages, you're in for both a shock and a treat because Microsoft® Visual Web Developer™ comes with the same source code editor as high-end versions of Microsoft Visual Studio®.

Source code, in this sense, doesn't necessarily mean ASP.NET program code. In Visual Web Developer, source code includes HTML, CSS, XML, JavaScript that runs on the browser, and so forth. This means you're almost certain to encounter the source code editor, and more likely sooner than later.

Fortunately, despite its power, the Visual Studio text editor is very easy to use. Once you understand its key features, you'll quickly

NOTE

Occasionally, even the most dedicated advocates of WYSIWYG editing work directly with code.

start creating more code with fewer keystrokes and fewer errors than ever before. To help you, this chapter begins with an introduction to the Visual Studio (and therefore the Visual Web Developer) text editor.

The chapter's final section explains your options for storing any ASP.NET program code you do write and for compiling a site before or after you copy it to another server. However, neither this chapter nor this book provide an introduction to programming. If that's what you need, consider a more detailed book such as *Microsoft ASP.NET 2.0 Programming Step By Step* from Microsoft Press®.

Using the Text Editor

Visual Web Developer can open any file in your site in text mode (provided, of course, that the file is textual).

TO OPEN A FILE IN TEXT MODE

1 Open or create the file as Chapter 6 directed.

2 If the Source tab at the bottom of the editing window is present but not selected, select it.

Figure 7-1 shows how Visual Web Developer displays an ASP. NET Web page in Source view.

Even though Source view is in effect, the Toolbox, the Quick Tag Toolbar, and the Properties window are enabled and working. For example, you can:

- Add controls by dragging them from the Toolbar and dropping them onto your source code.

- Select tags by clicking their icons in the Quick Tag Toolbar.

- View and modify control properties by using the Properties window.

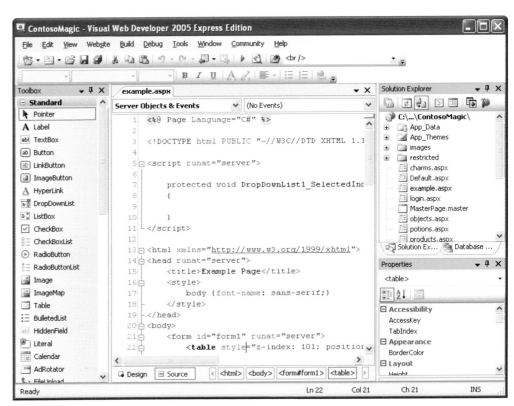

Figure 7-1
The Visual Web Developer text editor abounds with powerful features. For starters, note the color coding, the line numbering, and the collapsible brackets.

NOTE

If Visual Web Developer supports only one editing mode for a given type of file, it doesn't display editing mode tabs at the bottom of the editing window.

MORE INFO

To configure the way the text editor displays your code, choose Options from the Tools menu. Then, when the Options dialog box appears, open the Text Editor node in the tree view box at the left.

The editor automatically displays line numbers and also displays different types of code in different colors. In the figure, for example, HTML tag names are dark red, attribute names are bright red, attribute values are blue, and ordinary text is black. Similar conventions apply to CSS, program, and other kinds of code.

Using Outlining

For many kinds of source code, Visual Web Developer can collapse and expand blocks of code. This reduces clutter and scrolling and makes it easier to work with only the code that concerns you at the moment. Figure 7-2 shows outlining in action.

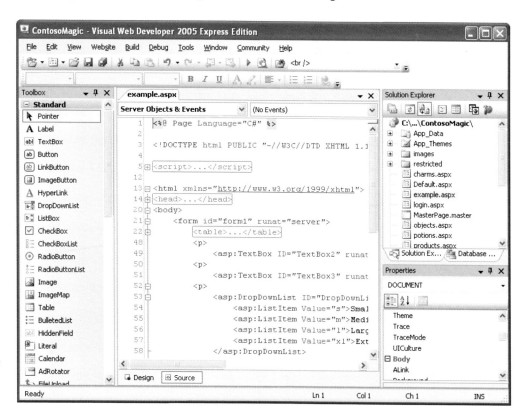

Figure 7-2
Collapsed blocks of code begin at lines 5, 14, and 22. This accounts for the breaks in line numbering and for the plus -sign (+) Expand icons.

In this figure:

- Lines 5-11 contain a <script> . . . </script> block, but the developer previously clicked the Collapse icon, a minus sign (-), that appears on line 5 of Figure 7-1. This tells the editor not to display the contents of the block.

    If the developer wants to view or modify the block, he or she would simply click the Expand icon (+) that now appears on line 5.
- Lines 14-19 contain the <head> . . . </head> section of the Web page. The developer has collapsed this as well.
- Lines 22-47 contain the code for an HTML table, but the developer collapsed this block, too.
- The developer could also collapse:

    - The <asp:DropDownList> . . . <asp:DropDownList> block on lines 53-58.
    - The <p> . . . </p> block on lines 52-59.
    - The <form> . . . </form> block on lines 21-60.
    - The <body> . . . </body> block on lines 20-61.
    - The <html> . . . </html> block on lines 13-62.

    In each case, the developer would click the minus icon (-) that appears just to the right of the starting line number.

If you run a Find or Replace command on a file that contains collapsed blocks, you can choose whether or not to search the hidden text. If you do search hidden text and find a match, the editor will expand any collapsed blocks that contain it.

Using Split View

Like Microsoft Office programs, Visual Web Developer can split the editing window into two panes that you can scroll independently. This makes it easy to work on two blocks of code at once or to view one block while working on another. To use this feature, either:

- Use the mouse to grab the split handle that appears just above the editing window's vertical scroll bar and drag it to the location you want. (The split handle looks like a tiny unlabeled button or "bump.")

- Select some text or set the insertion point inside the editing window. Then, choose Split from the Window menu.

To return to single pane view, either:

- Drag the split bar back to its original position at the top of the window.

- Choose Remove Split from the Window menu.

    Figure 7-3 shows Split view in effect.

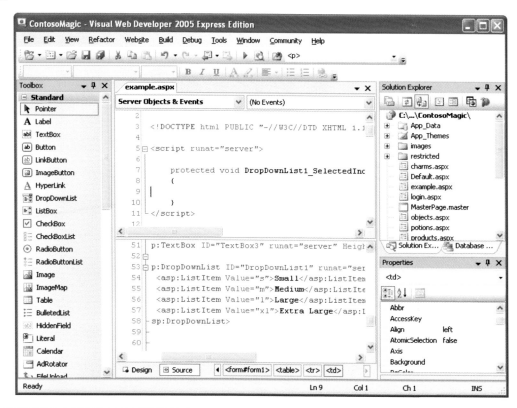

Figure 7-3
In Split mode, the editor displays two different sections of the same file.

Using Go To, Bookmarks, and the Task List

The text editor can position its display at any line number you want. To use this feature, first choose Go To from the Edit menu or press Ctrl+G. Then, type the line number you want and click OK.

Bookmarks provide another way of moving rapidly to the code you want. To use this feature, you set a bookmark at the beginning of each block of code you're editing, and then use shortcut keys, toolbar buttons, or menu commands to jump forward or backward through the bookmarks. The Text Editor toolbar and the Edit menu (under Bookmarks) provide a variety of commands for setting, positioning to, and clearing bookmarks.

The task list stores reminders of work you need to do. To add such a reminder for a specific line of code, select the line of code, then choose Bookmarks from the Edit menu and click Add Task List Shortcut. To come back to that line of code use the following procedure.

TIP

Visual Web Developer bookmarks have no direct relation to HTML bookmarks that you define with <a name="*bookmark*"> tags.

TO USE A TASK LIST SHORTCUT

1 Choose **Task List** from the View menu.

2 When the Task List window appears, choose **Shortcuts** in the drop-down list near the top.

3 The lower part of the window will display a list of shortcuts you've saved.

- To position the editor at the line for any task, double-click that task.

- To mark a task as complete, select the check box in the second column.

- To delete a task, select it and press the Delete key.

NOTE

Visual Web Developer remembers bookmarks and task list shortcuts from one editing session to the next.

Figure 7-4 shows Visual Web Developer displaying a page with two bookmarks and one task list shortcut.

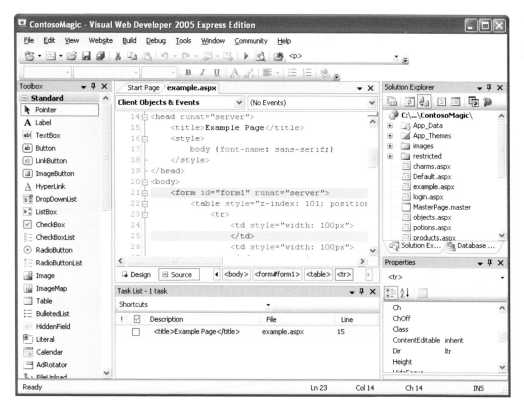

Figure 7-4
The blue shading on lines 21 and 25 indicates bookmarks. The Task List window displays an open task for line 15.

Making Sense of IntelliSense

Wouldn't it be great if your text editor keyed in most of your tag names, attribute names, attribute values, apostrophes, and closing tags for you? And if, along the way, it constantly coached you with lists of possible choices? Well, that's what the IntelliSense® feature does.

NOTE

The terms *code completion* and *statement completion* also refer to IntelliSense. However, the word *IntelliSense* is a Microsoft trademark.

Suppose, for example, you're entering HTML code. When you type the opening angle bracket (<) for a tag, IntelliSense displays a selection list of valid tag names as shown in Figure 7-5.

Figure 7-5
When working with HTML, typing a
tag's opening angle bracket causes
IntelliSense to display a selection list
of valid tag names.

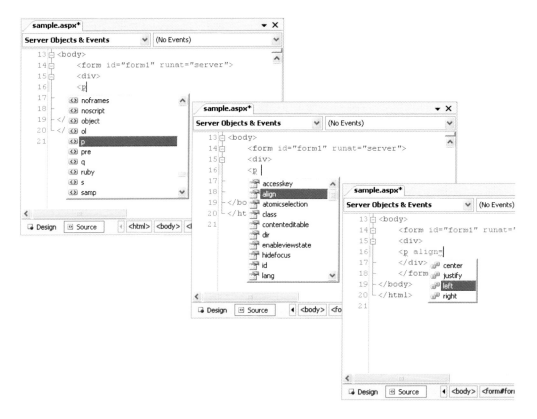

If you continue to type, IntelliSense positions the selection list at the first matching entry. In the figure, for example:

■ The developer has typed **p**. Therefore, IntelliSense has positioned the list to the first entry beginning with *p*.

■ If the developer then typed **r**, IntelliSense would position to the first entry beginning with *pr*, and so forth.

TIP

To configure IntelliSense processing, choose Options from the Tools menu. When the Options dialog box appears, open the Text Editor node, select a file type, and choose the options you want under the Statement Completion heading at the right.

You can also select an item from the IntelliSense list by using the mouse to scroll through the list and then clicking the entry you want.

Once you've typed or selected the tag name you want, add it to the page by taking *one* of these three actions:

■ Double-click the correct tag name in the selection list.

■ Press the Tab key.

■ Type any character that, according to the rules of HTML, marks the end of the tag name. For example, type a space or a closing angle bracket (>).

The lead-in for an HTML attribute is a space. If you type a space immediately after any tag name or attribute, a selection list of permissible attribute names will appear as shown in the middle of Figure 7-5.

To select an attribute name, repeat the procedure you used for the tag name. Then, type the equal sign (=) that leads into the attribute value. If the given attribute has a limited set of correct values, IntelliSense will display them in yet another selection list like the rightmost example in Figure 7-5.

When you type the tag's closing angle bracket (>), IntelliSense will automatically provide a closing tag. For example, when you type the closing angle bracket (>) at the end of <p align=left>, IntelliSense will automatically supply an </p> tag and set the insertion point between the opening and closing tags.

Note that IntelliSense lists appear because you type a lead-in (or trigger) character, such as an opening angle bracket (<) in HTML. If for some reason the selection list disappears, setting the cursor immediately after the lead-in character won't bring the drop-down list back. Instead you must either:

TIP

Using IntelliSense is always optional. If you ignore the IntelliSense list and key in an HTML tag (or anything else) completely by hand, IntelliSense won't interfere with the characters you enter.

■ Delete and re-enter the lead-in character (in this case, the opening angle bracket).

■ Choose IntelliSense from the Edit menu, and then choose List Members.

■ Press Ctrl+J.

Visual Web Developer supports IntelliSense not only for HTML, but also for XML, JavaScript, CSS, and all .NET programming languages.

Detecting Syntax Errors

As you enter your code, Visual Web Developer constantly checks for syntax errors. Then, for each error, it:

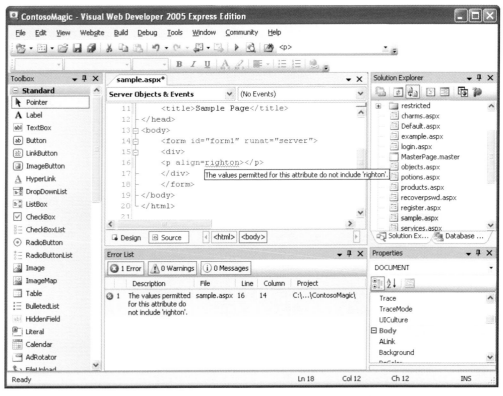

- Displays a red squiggly line under the bad code.

- Displays the error message, line number, and filename in an Error List window. If you double-click this message, the editor displays the problem line.

- Displays the error message as a tooltip if you hover the mouse over the bad code. Figure 7-6 shows how this looks in practice.

 To choose the browser version or HTML specification (that is, the *schema*) you want to use for creating and validating Web pages, follow the next procedure.

Figure 7-6
Visual Web Developer detects and highlights syntax errors in your source code.

TO CHOOSE AN HTML SCHEMA

1 Choose Options from the Tools menu.

2 When the Options dialog box appears, open Text Editor, HTML, and Validation in the tree view box at the left.

3 Select the browser or HTML specification you want from the Target drop-down list at the right.

You can also choose a browser version or HTML specification by using the drop-down list on the HTML Source Editing toolbar.

TIP
To display the HTML Source Editing toolbar, choose Toolbars from the View menu, and then choose HTML Source Editing.

Finding and Replacing Text

Visual Web Developer provides extremely powerful commands for finding and searching text.

TO USE FIND AND REPLACE COMMANDS

1 Choose Find And Replace from the Edit menu.

2 Choose one of the available subcommands. This will display a Find And Replace dialog box like those shown in Figure 7-7.

3 Visual Web Developer offers five Find And Replace commands. If you discover that you've chosen the wrong command, use the drop-down lists at the top of the dialog box to select the one you want.

Figure 7-7
Here are two forms of the Search And Replace
dialog box. The form at the left performs a Quick
Find; the one at the right performs a Find And
Replace In Files.

The five Find And Replace commands are:

- **Quick Find** Searches for all occurrences of a given string in the current document, the current selection, all open documents, or the current project. Two modes of searching are available.

  - **Find Next** Advances sequentially to the next occurrence of the given text each time you click a Find Next button or (if you've closed the Find And Replace dialog box) each time you press F3.

  - **Bookmark All** In one operation, sets a Visual Web Developer bookmark on each line that contains the given text. This mode, however, isn't available when using Quick Find to search an entire Web site

MORE INFO

For more information about Visual
Web Developer bookmarks, refer
to the section titled, "Using Go
To, Bookmarks, and the Task List"
earlier in this chapter.

- **Quick Replace** Works like Quick Find, but optionally replaces each occurrence of the Find text with given Replace text. Use these commands to move through each search result:

  - **Find Next** Advances to the next occurrence of the Find text. No replacement occurs.

  - **Replace** Replaces the current instance of the Find text, then advances to the next occurrence.

  - **Replace All** Searches the entire scope for the Find text and replaces each instance with the Replace text. When this process is complete, the editor will display an unsaved version of each changed file. This is so you can undo the Replace All or save only the files you want.

- **Find In Files** Searches for all occurrences of a given string in the current document, all open documents, or the current Web site. You can also restrict the search by filename extension. This command differs from Quick Find in two primary ways:

  - Unlike Quick Find, this command can't search for occurrences one at a time. It always performs a Search All.

  - The Find In Files command doesn't open any files that contain the given text. Instead, it lists the filename and line number of each instance in your choice of two windows: Find Results 1 or Find Results 2.

TIP
To display any line reported in the Find Results 1 or Find Results 2 window, double-click that report line.

- **Replace In Files** Searches for text just like the Find In Files command, but opens each file that contains the Find text and replaces it with text you specify.

  Like the Find In Files command, Replace In Files reports each instance of the Find text in either the Find Results 1 or Find Results 2 window (your choice).
  Like the Quick Replace command, Replace In Files leaves these files open and doesn't save them. That way, you can undo the changes or save only the files you want.

- **Find Symbol** Searches for text contained in symbol names you assign to variables, pro-cedure names, and other programming items. It won't find instances of the Find text that appear in comments or literals.

Formatting Source Code

When you add, relocate, configure, or delete Web page controls in Design view, Visual Web Developer naturally updates your HTML code. In so doing, it follows predefined rules for indenting certain tags, adding line breaks, and otherwise formatting its code.

Most developers want Visual Web Developer to use the same rules they follow when editing HTML by hand. If Visual Web Developer isn't formatting HTML the way you want, proceed as follows.

TO SET RULES FOR HTML FORMATTING

1 Choose Options from the Tools menu.

2 When the Options dialog box shown in Figure 7-8 appears, open the Text Editor and HTML nodes in the tree view at the left.

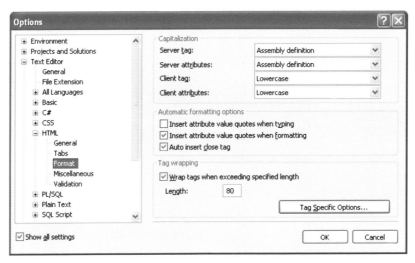

Figure 7-8
This panel of the Options dialog box configures the format of all HTML tags and server controls.

3 Select each node under HTML and review the settings that appear at the right. These nodes are:

■ **General** Controls options for displaying HTML in Source view. This pertains to options—like statement completion (IntelliSense), word wrapping, and line numbers—that have no effect on the saved HTML.

■ **Tabs** Controls the standard unit of indentation. For example, you can choose whether or not to indent, how much to indent, and whether to use spaces or tab characters for indenting.

■ **Format** Controls the capitalization of tag and attribute names, automatic insertion of quotation marks, automatic insertion of closing tags, and insertion of line breaks for tags that exceed a specified length. These controls are visible in Figure 7-8.

■ **Miscellaneous** Controls whether Visual Web Developer will assign a unique id= attribute to each control it pastes and whether it reformats any HTML it pastes.

■ **Validation** Controls which HTML specification Visual Web Developer will use when syntax-checking your code and what kind of errors you want it to report.

4 To configure the formatting and display options for a specific tag, click the **Format** node under HTML and then click the **Tag Specific Options** button. This displays the Tag Specific Options dialog box shown in Figure 7-9.

5 In the tree view box at the left, select the tag name you want to configure, then use the controls at the right to specify the settings you want. For example, specify whether the tag usually has a separate closing tag (like <p> . . . </p>), whether to insert line breaks before and after the tag, whether to indent the tag contents, whether to enable outlining, and what color to use when displaying the tag.

6 Click the **OK** button to save your changes.

TIP

If you want to reformat some existing HTML code, select it in Source view, then right-click the selection and choose Format Selection from the shortcut menu. To select the entire page, press Ctrl+A.

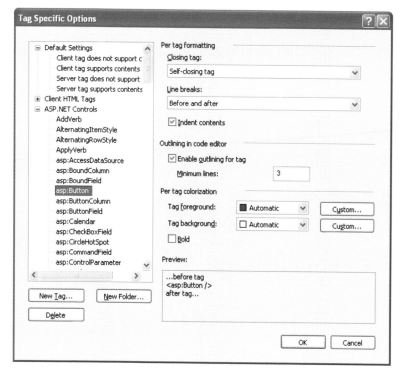

Figure 7-9
This dialog box configures the format of individual HTML tags and server controls.

Locating More Editing Commands

The Edit menu provides a number of useful commands on its Advanced submenu. To use any of these commands, select the code you want to modify, choose Advanced from the Edit menu, and then select the command you want.

The HTML Source Editing Toolbar provides rapid access to six commands that previous sections have already described. To display or hide this toolbar, choose Toolbars from the View menu and then choose HTML Source Editing.

The Text Editor Toolbar provides buttons for four IntelliSense commands, four text editing commands, and eight bookmarking commands. Unlike the HTML Source Editing toolbar, this toolbar works with any type of code. To display it, choose Toolbars from the View menu, and then choose Text Editor.

Storing, Compiling, and Publishing Program Code

Sooner or later, most Web site developers write Microsoft Visual Basic® .NET, C#, or J# program code that runs on the Web server. If and when you do this, you can choose either of two places to store your program code.

- **In-Line** With this approach, the program code for a Web page resides in the same file as the HTML. Specifically, it resides between <script runat="server"> and </script> tags.

  To use this approach, make sure the Place Code In Separate File check box is cleared when you create a new Web page and the Add New Item dialog box appears.

- **Code Behind** In this scenario, you store your HTML code and your program code in different files. For example, the HTML could be in an .aspx file, and the C# code in a .cs file.

  To use this approach, select the Place Code In Separate File check box.

NOTE

This section presumes that you have a working knowledge of ASP. NET programming. If you don't, you should probably move on to the next chapter. You don't need this material to understand the rest of the book.

If you choose the Code Behind approach, the @ Page directive at the top of the new page will contain *CodeFile* and *Inherits* attributes as shown below:

```
<%@ Page Language="C#" AutoEventWireup="true"
        CodeFile="mypage.aspx.cs" Inherits="mypage" %>
```

The *CodeFile* attribute specifies the name of the file that contains the program source code. The *Inherits* attribute specifies the class name coded as follows in C#:

```
public partial class mypage : System.Web.UI.Page
{
}
```

or like this in Visual Basic .NET:

```
Partial Class mypage
        Inherits System.Web.UI.Page
```

TIP

If you move the code-behind file to another folder, you must correct the *CodeFile* attribute in the @ *Page* directive.

If you rename the .aspx file, you must also rename the code-behind file and rename the code-behind class name.

If all your program source code resides in-line, or in a folder named *app_code* just inside your site's root, you don't have to *build* (or compile) your site before running it locally or copying it to another server. ASP.NET will compile each file the first time a Web visitor requests a page that needs it. This saves you a step, but it means that your program source code must be present on any Web server that runs your site.

If your program source code resides anywhere else, you'll need to choose Build Web Site from the Build menu, and then be sure to upload the resulting */bin* folder along with the rest of your site. You won't, however, need to upload your program source files; this may reduce the risk of theft or tampering.

In Summary...

When editing source code such as HTML, XML, CSS, and program code, Visual Web Developer uses the same professional editor as full versions of Visual Studio. This gives you full access to professional editing features such as color coding, outlining, split view, going to a line number, bookmarking, a task list, IntelliSense, syntax checking, and code formatting.

The next chapter explains when it might be attractive to create your own server controls and then how to do just that.

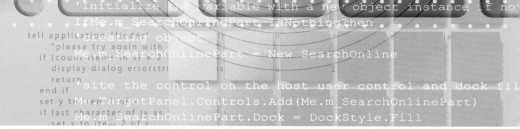

Chapter 8

Creating and Using Web User Controls

Web pages in the same site often use standard visual components such as headers, menu bars, and footers. Typically, these components are identical, or nearly so, from page to page. This unifies the site and improves overall continuity.

Most experienced developers develop such components once, then use the results on multiple pages. This guarantees uniformity and simplifies maintenance. When later changing the site, the developer updates one central copy and the results appear on each page.

Microsoft® ASP.NET 2.0, and therefore Microsoft Visual Web Developer™, have two features that are especially useful for implementing standardized content.

- **Web User Controls** Display areas of standard or programmed content within a page.

- **Master Pages** Fill an entire page with standard or programmed content, except for one or more open areas where variable content can appear.

The rest of this chapter will explain how to create and use Web user controls. The next chapter will explain when and how to use master pages.

Creating and Designing Web User Controls

Any time you want the same content (or nearly the same content) to appear within multiple pages, consider using a Web user control. Creating one of these controls is almost like creating a Web page.

CREATING A WEB USER CONTROL

1 In Visual Web Developer, open the site that will display the user control.

2 Choose **New File** from the File menu.

3 When the Add New Item dialog box appears, fill out these form fields:

■ **Templates** Select Web User Control.

■ **Name** Specify a filename for the control. The default and required filename extension is .ascx.

■ **Language** Choose the language for any program code you plan to write: Microsoft Visual Basic®, Visual C#®, or Visual J#®. When in doubt, choose the same language that you used for the rest of the site.

■ **Place Code In Separate File** Select this box if you want to keep the HTML code and the program code for this control in separate files. Clear it to keep both kinds of code in the .ascx file.

4 Click the **Add** button to create the control.

You add controls to a Web user control just as you'd add them to a Web page: You can drag them from the Toolbox, insert them using the Layout menu, or use any other method that Chapter 6 described. The following procedure, for example, creates a Web user control that displays the current date.

TO CREATE A WEB USER CONTROL TO DISPLAY THE CURRENT DATE

1 Using the four-step procedure described above, create a new Web user control named **TodayIs.ascx**.

2 Display the *TodayIs.ascx* control in Design view.

3 Set the insertion point in the top left corner of the editing window, then type **Today is:**

4 Look in the Standard toolbox group and find the icon for a *Literal* control. Drag this icon out of the Toolbox and drop it after the text from step 3 (Today is:).

5 Make sure the Properties window displays properties for the new *Literal* control: **Literal1** System.Web.UI.WebControls.Literal.

6 Using the properties window, change the value of the *ID* property from *Literal1* to *litTodayIs*.

7 Click in the main editing window, then press **F7**. This displays the Web user control's program code in Source view.

8 Two drop-down lists should now appear at the top of the editing window.

■ For Visual Basic .NET, select Page in the left drop-down list and Load in the right drop-down list. Then, type the statement shown below in green (Visual Web Developer supplies the code shown in normal text).

```
Protected Sub Page_Load(ByVal sender As Object, _

        ByVal e As System.EventArgs)

    litTodayIs.Text = DateTime.Today.ToLongDateString

End Sub
```

■ For C#, select TodayIs in the left drop-down list and Page_Load(object sender, EventArgs e) in the right drop-down list. Then, type the statement shown below in green (Visual Web Developer supplies the code shown in normal text).

```
protected void Page_Load(object sender, EventArgs e)

{

    litTodayIs.Text = DateTime.Today.ToLongDateString();

}
```

The statement you type gets the current date from the operating system, formats it for display, and stores the result in the *Literal* control you added in steps 4, 5, and 6.

9 Choose **Save TodayIs.ascx** from the File menu to save the control. The next section will explain how to test it.

Adding Web User Controls to a Page

You can add a Web user control to any ASP.NET Web page in the same site. The procedure is remarkably simple.

TO ADD A WEB USER CONTROL TO AN ASP.NET WEB PAGE

1 Open the ASP.NET page that you want to display the Web user control.

2 Drag the Web user control from the Solution Explorer window and drop it in place on the open Web page.

TIP

You can also add one Web user control to another Web user control.

To test the Web user control, right-click any page that contains the control and choose View In Browser from the shortcut menu. This should produce results like those shown in Figure 8-1.

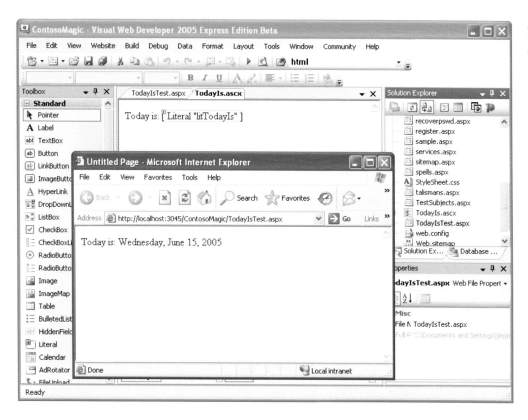

Figure 8-1
To test a Web user control, display a page that contains it.

Using Web User Controls Effectively

Web user controls are generally easy to use. Nevertheless, problems can arise. The topics in this section answer some common questions and provide advice for dealing with some typical problems.

Understanding Web User Control Tags

The first time you add a given Web user control to a page, Visual Web Developer adds two tags:

- **An @ *Register* Tag** This tag appears above the HTML source code for the page. It associates a Web user control's filename with a tag prefix and name. Here's an example:

```
<%@ Register Src="TodayIs.ascx"
    TagName="TodayIs" TagPrefix="uc1" %>
```

A Web user control needs only one such declaration per page, even if the control appears several times.

- **A Web User Control Tag** This tag appears where you want the Web user control to appear on the page. The tag prefix and name from the @ *Register* declaration identify the type of control. Here's an example:

```
<uc1:TodayIs ID="TodayIs1" runat="server" />
```

A page requires one tag like this for each instance of the Web user control it displays.

Of course the browser doesn't receive either the @ Register directive or the Web user control tag. These tags simply tell ASP.NET to load a Web user control object into memory on the Web server.

When ASP.NET sends the page to the Web visitor, it tells the Web user control object to render itself as HTML. This HTML, and not the original tag, is what ASP.NET sends to the Web visitor.

Using CSS Styles in Web User Controls

When designing a Web user control, keep in mind that ASP.NET will merge the control's output into the <body> section of any Web page that uses the control. As a result, the Web user control has no <head> section of its own, no <body> and </body> tags, and so forth.

This is particularly noticeable if, like most experienced Web developers, you use CSS styles to format your pages. Because page-specific styles and links to shared style sheet files usually reside in the <head> section, your style rules generally won't be available when you design a Web user control. This leads to a less-than WYSIWYG experience. There are two alternatives for dealing with this issue:

- Apply CSS styles as usual, ignoring the fact that they don't seem to be taking effect. To check the control's finished appearance, browse a page that contains it.

- Add a <style></style> block, links to shared style sheets, or both to the Web user control. This will make editing easier, but it may add redundant or unwanted styles to pages that use the control.

Keep in mind that when several pages use the same user control, each page can have its own styles. In such cases, a Web user control that uses CSS styles takes on the appearance of each page. This is one reason that Visual Web Developer doesn't try to apply default CSS styles to Web user controls.

Adjusting Relative URLs

When several pages use the same Web user control and those pages reside in different folders, relative URLs that work for one page may not work in another. For example:

- For a page that resides in the application root, displaying the company logo might require this tag:

```
<img src="images/logo.gif">
```

- For a page that resides in an application subfolder, displaying the same logo would require this tag:

```
<img src="../images/logo.gif">
```

This is a problem if you hard-code relative locations in <img src="..."> and <a href="...">
tags within a Web user control. Any relative path you code will be wrong if the Web page
using the control resides in a different folder than you expect.

To avoid this, code any <img> and <a> tags that use relative paths with runat="server"
attributes, and begin the relative location with a tilde (~) and a slash (/). Here are some
examples:

```
<a href="~/companyinfo.aspx" runat="server">
<img src="~/images/logo.gif" runat="server"></a>
```

When ASP.NET renders these controls, it replaces the tildes (~) with the path to the
application root. If, for example, the root is /myapplication, the tags will look like this when
the browser receives them:

```
<a href="/myapplication/companyinfo.aspx">
<img src="/myapplciation/images/logo.gif"></a>
```

Because the href= and src= locations are now relative to the application root, they'll
work correctly wherever the pages reside.

Coding Attributes for Web User Controls

The program code in a Web user control can make use of attributes you code in the tag that
loads the control. For example, you could write the program code for the *TodayIs* control in
Visual Basic .NET like this:

```
Public DateFormat As String


Protected Sub Page_Load(ByVal sender As Object,
    ByVal e As System.EventArgs)
  If LCase(DateFormat) = "short" Then
    litTodayIs.Text = DateTime.Today.ToShortDateString()
  Else
    litTodayIs.Text = DateTime.Today.ToLongDateString()
  End If
End Sub
```

NOTE

Declaring a variable or function as
Public (or, in C#, as *public*) makes
it accessible outside the class that
declares it. *Private* (or *private*)
variables and functions are only
accessible within the class that
declares them.

Because it's *Public*, the *DateFormat* variable will receive the value of any *DateFormat=* attribute you code on the tag that loads the control. In the following example, the first *<uc2: TodayIsVb>* tag displays a long date (the default) and the second displays a short date.

```
<%@ Register Src="TodayIs.ascx" TagName="TodayIs" TagPrefix="uc2" %>
<uc2:TodayIsVb ID="TodayIsVb1" runat="server" />
<uc2:TodayIsVb ID="TodayIsVb2"runat="server" DateFormat="short" />
```

If you know how to write the necessary Visual Basic or C# program code, you can also use public properties this way.

In Summary...

Web user controls provide a quick and easy way of creating content once and using it on multiple Web pages. To create a Web user control, you start from a Web User Control template and then add content just as you would to a complete Web page. To include the control's content on an ASP.NET page, first open the page in Design view, then drag the control from Solution Explorer and drop it into place. Web user controls have a .ascx file-name extension.

The next chapter will explain how to use Master Pages, another means of replicating content to many pages.

Chapter 9

Using Master Pages to Centralize Page Layout

Web user controls are very useful for designing repetitive layouts once and then using them in many pages. Their strength lies in replicating parts of pages; they're not as useful for replicating the layout of an entire page. To understand why this is so, consider the structure of an overall site design:

- The predominant design elements usually occupy the edges of each page. Web user controls usually reside in the middle of the page or along a small portion of one edge.

- A site-level design often includes style sheet files, scripts, and other elements that should appear in the <head> section of each page. Web user controls don't have a <head> section and unless you do some complex programming, Web user controls don't affect the <head> section of the pages that contain them.

Master Pages, a new feature of ASP.NET 2.0, are much better than Web user controls for controlling the overall appearance of a site. Master pages control every aspect of a page *except* those areas you designate to present variable content. Master pages are true page templates, not just page segments.

A *content page* is any page that uses a master page. Each time a visitor requests a content page, ASP.NET loads the master page, merges in whatever the content page provides, and sends the combined result to the Web visitor. Merging the master page and the content page on the fly (that is, every time a visitor requests the page) has two important consequences.

- The visitor always receives current versions of both the master page content and the content page content.
- The merged page has all the capabilities of any conventional ASP.NET page. For example, master pages, content pages, or both can contain whatever server controls or custom programming you want. This means you can customize any part of the page on the fly every time a visitor requests the page.

Creating a Master Page

The best time to plan master pages is when you start planning a new site. In this book, the site will be a for a fictitious business named Contoso Magic. Hypothetically, this business provides equipment and services for stage magicians. To create this site using master pages, follow these steps.

TO CREATE A SITE USING MASTER PAGES

1 Use the instructions in Chapter 3 to create a new site in a folder named ContosoMagic.

If you wish to follow the examples precisely, create a file system Web site. However, a local or remote IIS Web site will work as well.

2 Delete any Web pages the site contains. For example, delete the default.aspx page that Microsoft Visual Web Developer™ creates by default.

3 In the Server Explorer window, right-click the site's root folder (\ContosoMagic\) and choose **Add New Item** from the shortcut menu.

4 When the Add New Item dialog box appears, fill it out like this:

■**Templates** Select Master Page

■**Name** Accept the default name MasterPage.master.

■**Language** Choose your favorite programming language: Microsoft® Visual Basic®, Visual C#®, or Visual J#®. The sample code uses Visual C#.

■**Place Code In Separate File** To reproduce the sample site, clear this box.

5 Click the **Add** button to create the master page,.

Figure 9-1
A new master page contains only one element: a ContentPlaceHolder control that receives variable content.

By default, Visual Web Developer creates a master page that's blank except for one *ContentPlaceHolder* control. This type of control reserves space for variable content. Figure 9-1 illustrates the default master page.

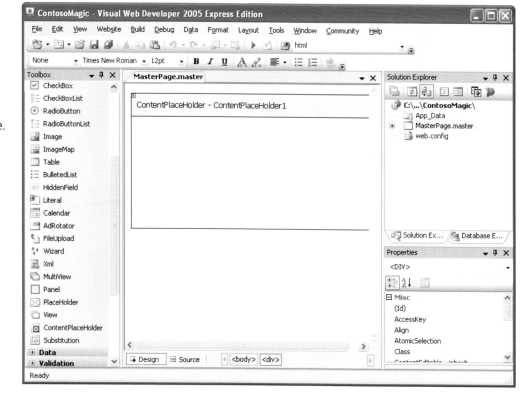

TIP
If you wish, you can delete the default *ContentPlaceHolder* control, add other *ContentPlaceHolder* controls, or do both. Each master page, however, must have at least one *ContentPlaceHolde* control. The Toolbox icon for a *ContentPlaceHolde* control appears in the Standard group, near the bottom.

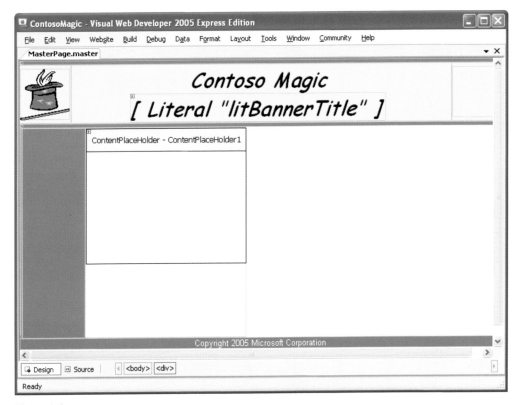

Figure 9-2 shows the completed master page for the Contoso Magic site. For a real site, you'd probably want to develop something more attractive but this simple design is enough to show the capabilities of Visual Web Developer.

Designing a master page is very much like designing a normal ASP.NET page. All the techniques from Chapters 6 and 7 apply. The sample design uses three HTML tables, each with *border* and *cellspacing* set to zero (0) and *width* set to 100 percent.

The first table displays the page banner. It has three rows and three columns, used as follows:

Figure 9-2
You can design master pages just as you would individual content pages. However, you must include at least one ContentPlaceHolder control on each master page.

- All three cells in the first row are merged. The merged cell displays a 5x5 pixel transparent GIF file. This reduces the row height below that of a default * * character. A CSS rule named *bordertxt* controls the background and font color.

- In the middle row:

  - The left cell displays an 80x80 pixel logo file named magichat.gif.

  - The middle cell displays the constant text Contoso Magic, a line break, and a *Literal* server control named *litBannerTitle*.

  - The right cell displays a transparent GIF file stretched to 80x80 pixels. This ensures that the left and right cells are the same size, and consequently that the middle cell is always centered in the browser window.

MORE INFO

For information about creating CSS rules, refer to Chapter 10, "Using Cascading Style Sheets".

For all three cells, a CSS rule named *bannertxt* establishes the typeface, font size, and background color.

■ The third row duplicates the first row.

The *litBannerTitle* control displays the textual name of each page. This name comes from a property named *Page.Title* that you assign for each content page. (The next section will explain this further.)

In Visual C#, copying the textual page name from the *Page.Title* property to the *litBannerTitle.Text* property requires the following code:

```
<script runat="server">

    protected void Page_Load(object sender, EventArgs e)

    {

        litBannerTitle.Text = Page.Title;

    }

</script>
```

In Visual Basic .NET, doing the same job requires this code:

```
<script runat="server">

    Protected Sub Page_Load(ByVal sender As Object, _

            ByVal e As System.EventArgs)

        litBannerTitle.Text = Page.Title

    End Sub

</script>
```

In each case:

■ The <script runat="server">...</script> tags define an in-line code block (that is, a block of code that resides within the Web page but executes on the Web server).

■ The next statement defines a *Page_Load* event handler. This event occurs (and triggers the event handler code) as soon as the page is completely loaded into memory and ready for work.

■ The third statement copies the *Page.Title* text into the *Text* property of the *litBannerTitle* control for eventual transmission to the browser.

The second table also contains three columns, but only one row. Here's how each column is used.

- The first column has a width of 1 percent. It displays the same transparent GIF file as the first table, this time stretching it to 1 pixel wide and 325 pixels high. This provides a small left margin and keeps relatively empty pages from looking squashed The *bordertext* CSS rule provides the background and font colors.

- The second column will eventually contain a DHTML menu but for now it's empty. An HTML attribute sets its width to 1 percent, but the same transparent GIF file, now stretched to 100 pixels wide and one pixel tall, actually controls its width. The *bordertext* CSS rule provides the background and font colors.

- The third column, which contains the *ContentPlaceHolder* control, has a width of 98 percent. This is where the content of each page will appear.

SEE ALSO

For instructions on adding tables, pictures, and other objects to a page, refer to Chapter 6, "Creating and Modifying Web Pages."

The third table contains a single cell that displays the page footer. A CSS rule named *footertxt* controls its background color, font color, and font size.

Of course, you'll design your master pages to suit your own needs. The only requirement is that each master page must contain at least one *ContentPlaceHolder* control.

Applying Master Pages to Content Pages

The easiest and best way of using master pages is to specify them when you create a new page.

TO SPECIFY A MASTER PAGE

1 Open the site that contains the master page. (The new content page will also reside in this site.)

2 In Solution Explorer, right-click the folder where you want the new content page to reside, then choose **Add New Item** from the shortcut menu.

3 When the Add New Item dialog box appears, fill it out as Chapter 6 instructed. However, be sure to specify:

■ **Template:** Web Form.

■ **Select Master Page:** Selected.

4 Click the **Add** button. Then, when the Select A Master Page dialog box shown in Figure 9-3 appears, select the master page you want.

5 To create the page, click the **OK** button.

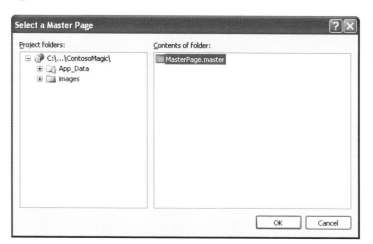

Figure 9-3
Use this dialog box to specify the master page that a new content page should use.

When you view the new page in Design view, the portions that come from the master page will be dimmed as shown in Figure 9-4. To modify anything in the dimmed part of the page, you must open and change the master page.

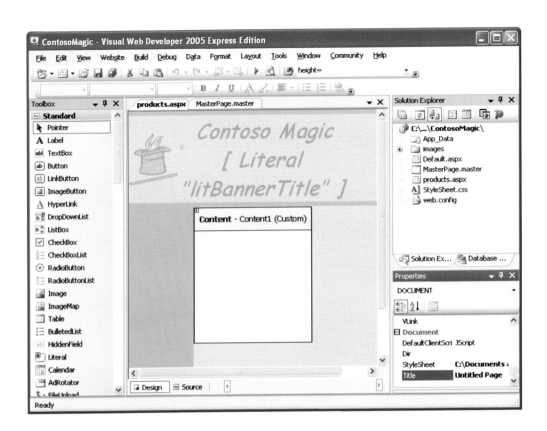

Figure 9-4
When you design a content page,
any master page portions appear
dimmed.

Figure 9-4 also shows a *Content* server control that's *not* dimmed. This is where you should add any content unique to the page. Don't worry if this area initially seems small; it expands to fit any content you add.

Note the *Title* property that appears in the Properties window. This is where you put the page title that the master page will copy into the *Literal*.control named *litBannerTitle*

Using Master Pages Effectively

Figure 9-5 shows a content page using the master page that the preceding sections explained how to develop. In addition, the page displays some preliminary content. To create such a page:

TO CREATE A PAGE SHOWING PRELINARY CONTENT

1 Create a page named products.aspx and configure it to use the master page named *MasterPage.master*. If necessary, refer to the procedures earlier in this chapter.

2 Type in the variable content, then save the page.

3 Right-click the page in Solution Explorer and choose **View In Browser** from the shortcut menu.

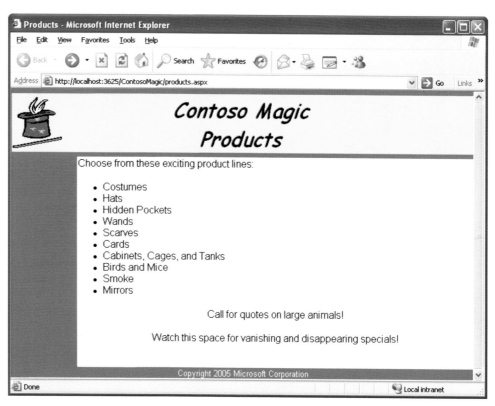

Figure 9-5
At the browser, content pages and master pages appear seamlessly integrated.

Looking Inside Master Pages

Content pages that use a master page initially contain very little source code. Here's a typical example:

```
<%@ Page Language="C#"
      MasterPageFile="~/MasterPage.master"
      Title="Products" %>
<asp:Content
      ID="Content1"
      ContentPlaceHolderID="ContentPlaceHolder1"
      Runat="Server">
</asp:Content>
```

The @ *Page* directive specifies the programming language for any ASP.NET program code you add to the page, the name of the master page file, and the page title.

The <asp:Content> tag specifies its own ID, the ID of a *ContentPlaceHolder* control in the master page, and the required *runat="server"* attribute. This provides a clue to the way master pages work:

- The master page contains one or more *ContentPlaceHolder* controls, each with its own ID.

- When a content page uses a master page, it should contain one *Content* control for each *ContentPlaceHolder* control in the master page.

- When a visitor requests the content page, ASP.NET merges the contents of each *Content* control into the corresponding *ContentPlaceHolder* control in the master page, then delivers the results.

Note that like a Web user control, a content page that uses a master page contains no <html></html> tags, no <head> section, no <body></body> tags, and no <form></form> tags. The master page supplies all of these.

Modifying Existing Pages to Use Master Pages

Visual Web Developer has no command or wizard that applies a master page to an existing Web page. Instead, you must follow this manual procedure.

TO APPLY A MASTER PAGE TO AN EXISTING WEB PAGE

1 Create a new content page that uses the master page you want.

2 Copy the content you want from the old page to the clipboard.

3 Paste the content from the clipboard into the new page.

4 Delete or rename the old content page, then rename the new one.

If you feel this approach omits something necessary from the page, or if you just like working in Source view, try this procedure.

TO APPLY A MASTER PAGE TO AN EXISTING WEB PAGE IN SOURCE VIEW

1 In Source view, delete everything from the opening <html> tag to the beginning of the content you want to retain. You must delete at least the <html> tag, the <head> section, the <body> tag, and any <form> tags.

2 Delete everything that comes after the content you want to retain. This must include at least any </form> tags, the </body> tag, and the </html> tag.

3 Enclose the retained content within <asp:Content> and </asp:Content > tags, making sure to code *ID=*, *ContentPlaceHolderID=*, and *runat="server"* attributes. The *ContentPlaceHolderID=* attribute must specify the name of a **ContentPlaceHolder** control in the master page.

4 Add a *MasterPageFile=* attribute to the @ Page directive, making sure that it points to the master page you want.

5 Test and refine.

Adjusting Relative URLs

As with Web user controls, you'll need to take precautions if Web pages in various folders will use the same master page. Specifically, code any <img src=""> and <a href=""> attributes relative to the site root, and precede the path with a tilde (~). Here's an example:

```
<img src="~/images/magichat.gif">
```

Modifying Header Information

Occasionally, you may want content pages to override settings that appear in the <head> section of a master page. To do this, add *runat="server"* to the <head> tag in the master page, and then add program code in each Web page to override the information you want to change. For example, in the master page, code:

```
<head runat="server">
```

and then in the content page, code the following in the *Page_Load* event handler. (The earlier section titled," Creating a Master Page," showed how to add a *Page_Load* event handler to a master page. The procedure for a content page is the same).

```
Master.Page.Header.Metadata.Add("keywords", "elephants")
```

This adds a tag like the following to the <head> section of the outgoing page.

```
<meta name="keywords" content="elephants">
```

NOTE

The *Master* object points to the master page, if any, that a content page is using.

In Summary...

ASP.NET master pages are essentially Web page templates. They typically supply formatting elements such as style sheets, headings, and footings.

Visitors don't browse master pages directly. Instead, they browse content pages that attach a master page. ASP.NET merges any unique content that the content page supplies into the master page, then it delivers the merged result to the visitor. This makes the site more uniform and easier to maintain.

The next chapter will explain how to create Cascading Style Sheet (CSS) files in Visual Web Developer.

Chapter 10

Using Cascading Style Sheets

Most experienced Web developers now use Cascading Style Sheets (CSS) to control typography, colors, and many other kinds of formatting within a site. The reasons are clear: Used properly, CSS provides much more flexibility and uniformity than older methods of page formatting.

Visual Web Developer™ provides a rich and easy-to-use environment for assigning CSS style rules to individual page elements and for creating shared style sheet files. This chapter introduces those features.

Formatting Page Elements Individually

To specify CSS styles for a specific page element, first select it in Design view and then either:

■ Choose Style from the Format menu or

■ Select the Style attribute in the Properties window, then click the ellipsis (. . .) button.

After you take either of these actions, Visual Web Developer displays the Style Builder dialog box shown in Figure 10-1.

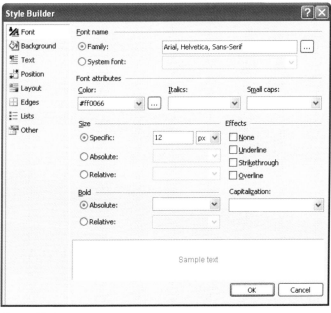

Figure 10-1
This dialog box applies CSS properties to page elements or to style sheet rules. Clicking any icon at the left displays a corresponding assortment of settings.

The eight categories along the left edge of the dialog box group the various CSS properties by type. The rest of the dialog box changes depending on the category you select. Most of these settings are fairly intuitive. If you find one that isn't, consult the built-in Help or browse the official CSS specifications at *http://www.w3.org/Style/CSS*

In Source view, Visual Web Developer provides IntelliSense® handling for styles within *style=* attributes. So, for example:

■ When you type **style="**, IntelliSense displays a selection list of CSS property names.

■ After you select or type a property name, type a colon (:). This triggers an IntelliSense display of acceptable property values.

■ When you finish selecting or typing the property value, type either the closing quote (") or a semicolon and a space (;) If you type a semicolon and a space, IntelliSense once again displays a list of CSS property names.

Using Named Styles Across Several Pages

Applying CSS properties to individual page elements provides plenty of flexibility but not much uniformity. The more pages the site contains, the harder the task of keeping fonts and colors uniform. Fortunately, CSS helps solve the problem with shared style sheet files.

Creating a New Style Sheet File

The procedure for creating a new style sheet file is very much like that for creating any other type of file.

TO CREATE A NEW STYLE SHEET FILE

1 Choose **New File** from the File menu or right-click a folder in Solution Explorer and select **Add New Item**.

2 When the Add New Item dialog box appears, select the **Style Sheet** template, override the default file name if you wish, and then click the **Add** button.

TIP
It's customary for style sheet files to reside in the Web site's root folder.

Creating Style Sheet Rules

In a style sheet file, each style rule must have a name (or more correctly, a *selector*). This is how Web pages refer to any style rules that the file contains.

A *style rule* consists of a name followed by a list of CSS properties and values. Table 10-1 lists the three types of style names.

Table 10-1
Types of CSS Style Names

World Wide Web Consortium	Visual Web Developer	Applies to
Type Selector	Element Name	All HTML elements of the corresponding type. For example, a style rule named *td* applies to the content of all <td> tags.
Class Selector	Class Name	All tags coded with a corresponding class= attribute. For example, a style rule named *.error* would apply to any tags you code with a *class="error"* attribute.
ID Selector	Element ID	All tags coded with a corresponding ID= attribute. For example, a style rule named *#btnSubmit* would apply to any tag coded *ID="btnSubmit"*.

TIP

When you *define* a style rule, a leading period (.) identifies a class selector and a leading pound sign (#) identifies an ID selector. However, you shouldn't code these leading characters when you *use* a style rule.

There are two ways of adding a named style rule to a style sheet file. They are:

- Type the style name, a space, and a pair of curly braces({}) on a new line at the end of the file, or between any two existing styles.

- Choose Add Style Rule from the Styles menu. This displays the Add Style Rule dialog box shown in Figure 10-2.

If you choose to use the Add Style Rule dialog box, continue as follows.

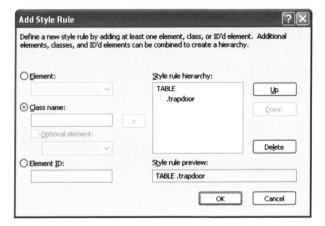

Figure 10-2
This dialog box creates new style rules. If you specify more than one name, the rule will only apply were all the names match.

TO USE THE ADD STYLE RULE DIALOG BOX

1 Select the type of style name you want: an Element, a Class Name, or an Element ID.

2 Choose or type the name you want.

3 If you're creating a class rule, you can restrict its scope to a certain tag name. For example, a style rule named *LI.presto* would apply only to tags coded <li class="presto">. To use this feature:

■ Specify the class name.

■ Select the Optional Element check box.

■ Select the tag name you want from the Optional Element drop-down list.

4 Click the right arrow button (>). This will add the new tag name to the Style Rule Hierarchy box.

5 Click the **OK** button to create the new style rule.

If you add several style names to the Style Rule Hierarchy box without clicking the OK button, Visual Web Developer will create a rule that applies only if *all* the given style names are in effect. If, for example, the Style Rule Hierarchy dialog box contains:

```
TABLE.links
    TD.external
        A.menu
```

The resulting style rule would apply only to tags that satisfy all these conditions:

■ The tag is an anchor (hyperlink) coded *class="menu"*.

■ The anchor resides within a table data cell coded *class="external"*.

■ The table data cell resides within a table coded *class="links"*.

The following HTML fragment illustrates this structure:

```
<TABLE class="links" ...>

    <TR ...>

        <TD class="external" ...>

            <A class="menu" ...>
```

Although the rules of HTML require the table row (<TR>) tag shown above, that tag is irrelevant to the *TABLE.links TD.external A.menu* style rule. That rule contains no requirements or restrictions based on <TR> tags.

A rule name such as *TABLE TR.shaded TD*, however, *would* be sensitive to <TR> tags. It would only apply to table data cells located within table rows coded *class="shaded"*, all within an HTML table.

Adding Properties to Style Sheet Rules

Once a style rule exists, you can add properties in any of these three ways:

- By typing (with the help of IntelliSense).
- By selecting the style rule and choosing Build Style from the Styles menu.
- By right-clicking the style rule and choosing Build Style from the shortcut menu.

Choosing Build Style displays the Style Builder dialog box that the earlier section, "Formatting Page Elements Individually," described. Fill out the dialog box as that section instructed, then click the OK button.

Figure 10-3 shows how Visual Web Developer displays the style sheet file for the Contoso Magic master page that appeared in the previous chapter. Note the CSS Outline window at the left. This window makes it easy to find and select styles located anywhere in the file.

NOTE

> Although Style sheet rules change the appearance of other objects, they have no appearance of their own. They're plain text, abstract specifications. That's why there's no Design view for style sheet files.

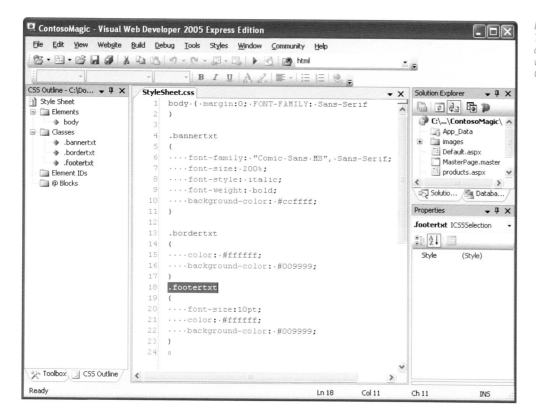

Figure 10-3
This is how Visual Web Developer displays
a typical style sheet file. If the CSS Outline
window doesn't appear, choose Document
Outline from the View menu.

Using Shared Styles in Your Web Pages

To use the style rules in a style sheet file, you must link the style sheet file and the Web page.

TO LINK THE STYLE SHEET FILE AND THE WEB PAGE

1 Open the Web page or master page that will use the shared style sheet file.

- Display the page in Design view, then drag the style sheet file from Solution Explorer and drop it onto the open page.

2 Take either of these actions:

- Select DOCUMENT in the Properties window, select the StyleSheet property, click the ellipsis (. . .) button, use the resulting dialog box to select the style sheet file you want, and then click OK.

Once you link the style sheet file and the page, any style rules with type or ID selectors (that is, any rules named after HTML tags or *ID=* attributes) will take effect immediately. To apply a class rule to an element, proceed as follows.

TIP

Many experienced Web developers never assign style attributes—particularly colors and font attributes—directly to a page element. Instead, they always use rules from shared style sheet files.

Although at first this approach might seem abstract and indirect, it produces sites that are much more uniform and much easier to maintain over time.

TO APPLY A CLASS RULE TO AN ELEMENT

1 Open the Web page or master page, then select the element in Design view.

2 In the Properties window, look for a property named *Class* or *CssClass*.

3 Type the name of the style as the *Class* or *CssClass* property value. Don't type a leading period.

In Summary...

Cascading Style Sheet (CSS) rules modify the properties of elements on a Web pages. Visual Web Developer can help you formulate these rules graphically (using dialog boxes) or as text (using IntelliSense).

Although you can specify CSS properties for individual page elements, storing CSS rules in style sheet files and linking those files to multiple pages (such as all the pages in your site) will impart a more uniform and professional appearance. Nevertheless, Visual Web Developer supports both methods of storing and applying styles.

The next chapter will explain how to create and use ASP.NET themes and skins, two more ways of centrally controlling a site's appearance.

Chapter 11

Controlling Appearance with ASP.NET Themes

The previous chapter explained how Cascading Style Sheets (CSS) control the appearance of HTML elements. CSS can control almost any visual aspect of an HTML element and, in the case of type selectors, it can do so without any additional code in the element itself. For example, a CSS rule named td automatically affects every <td> tag in the same page.

Unfortunately, the same approach doesn't work with ASP.NET Web server controls. CSS can affect any HTML code that a Web server control creates, but it can't affect the server control itself. To centrally control the appearance of Web server controls throughout a page or site, you need ASP.NET 2.0 *Themes*.

Themes are a new and powerful feature of Microsoft® ASP.NET 2.0. This chapter will explain how to use them.

> **NOTE**
> The Theme feature in ASP.NET 2.0 is a new technology. For example, it has nothing to do with the Themes features in Microsoft FrontPage® 2003, Microsoft Office XP, or Microsoft Windows® SharePoint® Services 1.0.

Creating ASP.NET Themes

Like CSS style sheets, a theme has no visual appearance of its own. Therefore you create a theme in the Microsoft Visual Web Developer™ text editor.

TO CREATE A THEME IN THE TEXT EDITOR

1 Open the Web site you want to control with a theme.

2 Right-click the site's root folder (such as \ContosoMagic\), choose **Add Folder** from the shortcut menu, and then select **Theme Folder** from the resulting submenu. At this point:

- If the site doesn't already contain an App_Themes folder, Visual Web Developer will create one.

- Visual Web Developer will always create a subfolder with a name like Theme1, but leave that name open for renaming.

3 Rename the new theme subfolder. The name you assign will become the theme name.

TIP

A Web site can contain as many themes as you want; just keep creating subfolders within App_Themes.

Of course, an empty theme folder will have no effect on your site. To control the appearance of your site, you must first add .skin or .css files. The next two sections explain how to do this.

Adding Skins to an ASP.NET Theme

In ASP.NET 2.0, a *skin file* specifies visual properties for one or more kinds of Web server control. A single theme subfolder can accommodate as few or as many skin files as you like. If there's more than one file, ASP.NET will read them all as if they were one file.

Skin files contain *skin tags*, which are XML code. The skin tag for each type of control should be familiar: it's the same as the tag that appears in a Web page.

Coding a skin file is slightly tedious because you have to do it in Source view and there's no IntelliSense® support.

TO CREATE A SKIN FILE

1 Right-click the theme subfolder where you want the skin file to reside, then choose **Add New Item** from the shortcut menu.

2 When the Add New Item dialog box appears, select the **Skin File** template, override the default file-name if you wish, and then click the **Add** button.

3 Visual Web Developer will display the new skin file in Source view.

4 Create a tag for each type of control you want the skin to affect. Here are some examples:

```
<asp:RadioButtonList runat="server" />

<asp:DropDownList runat="server" />

<asp:TextBox runat="server" />
```

These are the same tag names that appear when you add the corresponding Web server control to a Web page. If you're not sure what to type, open or create a Web page that contains the type of control you want, and look at the control's tag name in Source view.

Don't forget the *runat="server"* attribute and the closing slash (/) just inside the closing angle bracket.

5 Within each tag, add the server control attributes you want.

Again, these are the same attributes that the given control recognizes in a Web page. If you're not sure what to type, open or create a Web page that contains the type of control you want, configure the attribute you want, and then switch to Source view and look at the resulting code.

6 When you're done, choose **Save** from the file menu.

In general, a skin file can only affect the appearance of Web server controls. It *can't* control any of the following:

T I P

ASP.NET 2.0 Themes can contain both skin files and CSS files. If a skin file can't control the attribute or element you want, a CSS file might offer an alternative. The next section will explain how to use CSS files with ASP.NET 2.0 Themes

- ASP.NET user controls.

- Non-visual properties of Web server controls. For example, it can't control properties such as Click, SelectedIndexChanged, and EnableViewState.

- Web server controls such as <asp:Literal> that have no visual properties.

- HTML server controls.

- Ordinary HTML elements.

If necessary, you can define more than one skin tag for the same Web server control. Here's an example:

```
<asp:DropDownList BackColor="#rcr9d8" ForeColor="#0000cc"
    runat="server" />
<asp:DropDownList BackColor="#d0f0ff" ForeColor="#000000"
    runat="server" SkinId="skinDdlMirror" />
```

The first tag above is a *default skin* because it has no *SkinId=* attribute. The second is a *named skin* because it has a *SkinId=* attribute.

Suppose that these skins are part of a theme named *Smoke*, and that you have a Web page using that theme. In that page, the following <asp:DropDownList> tag, which has no *SkinId=* attribute, would get the first skin shown above.

```
<asp:DropDownList ID="ddlItem" runat="server">
    <asp:ListItem Value="a">Assistant</asp:ListItem>
    <asp:ListItem Value="b">Bird</asp:ListItem>
    <asp:ListItem Value="c">Coin</asp:ListItem>
    <asp:ListItem Value="e">Elephant</asp:ListItem>
    <asp:ListItem Value="w">Watch</asp:ListItem>
</asp:DropDownList>
```

Conversely, an <asp:DropDownList> tag coded *SkinId="skinDdlMirror"* would get the skin with that *SkinId*. For example:

```
<asp:DropDownList ID="ddlItem" runat="server"
        SkinId="skinDdlMirror">
    <asp:ListItem Value="a">Assistant</asp:ListItem>
    <asp:ListItem Value="b">Bird</asp:ListItem>
    <asp:ListItem Value="c">Coin</asp:ListItem>
    <asp:ListItem Value="e">Elephant</asp:ListItem>
    <asp:ListItem Value="w">Watch</asp:ListItem>
</asp:DropDownList>
```

To view any ASP.NET 2.0 theme, you must apply the theme to a Web page and then view the page in a browser. The section titled "Applying Themes to Pages and Sites" later in this chapter explains this procedure in detail.

Adding CSS Style Sheets to an ASP.NET Theme

If you wish, you can also store shared CSS style sheet files in your theme subfolders. ASP.NET will link these style sheets to any page that uses the given theme and has a *runat="server"* attribute in its <head> tag.

When you apply a theme like *Smoke* or *Mirrors* to a page or site, ASP.NET includes any CSS files that are part of the theme. It does this by adding <link> tags to the <head> section of the page, *after* any existing <link> tags. Suppose, for example, that you have:

- An App_Themes/Smoke folder that contains a CSS file named Smoke.css.

- An App_Themes/Mirrors folder that contains two CSS files named Mirrors.css and srorriM. css.

- A runat="server" attribute in each <head> tag, as in:

```
<head runat="server">

</head>
```

Then, ASP.NET will add the following style sheet link to any page that uses the *Smoke* theme:

```
<link href="App_Themes/Smoke/Smoke.css" text="text/css"
      rel="stylesheet" />
```

and these links to any page that uses the *Mirrors* theme:

```
<link href="App_Themes/Mirrors/Mirrors.css" text="text/css"
      rel="stylesheet" />
<link href="App_Themes/Mirrors/srorriM.css" text="text/css"
      rel="stylesheet" />
```

MORE INFO

Don't forget that ASP.NET 2.0 themes only control Web server controls. To centrally control the appearance of anything else, you still need to use CSS.

Because ASP.NET adds theme CSS links after any existing CSS links:

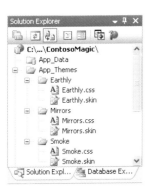

- Any CSS style rules or properties you code in a theme CSS file will override like-named rules or properties in CSS files you've manually linked to the page.

- If your site contains several themes, there's no need for the CSS files to duplicate each other. You can put the common rules and attributes in a conventionally-linked CSS file, and put just the overrides in theme CSS files.

The graphic at the left shows the arrangement of skin and CSS files for three themes in the ContosoMagic site. Although done here for clarity, there's no requirement that skin files, CSS files, and theme subfolders have similar names.

Applying Themes to Pages and Sites

You can apply themes to individual Web pages or to an entire site.

TO APPLY A THEME TO A SINGLE WEB PAGE

TIP

Themes you apply to individual pages override any theme you apply to the entire site.

1 Open the page in Visual Web Developer.

2 Display DOCUMENT in the Properties window.

3 Select the Theme property, then choose the theme you want from the drop-down list.

To specify a theme that applies to an entire Web site, you have to modify an XML file named web.config. Visual Web Developer creates this file whenever it creates a new site.

TO SPECIFY A DEFAULT THEME FOR ALL PAGES IN A SITE

1 Open the site's web.config file in Visual Web Developer.

2 Look for a pair of <system.web> and </system.web> tags. If present, these tags usually surround other content and appear right after the <configuration> tag. If your web.config file has no opening and closing <system.web> tags, create them.

3 Add the tag shown below in green after the <system.web> tag. Replace *Smoke* with the name of your theme.

```
<?xml version="1.0" encoding="utf-8"?>

<configuration xmlns="... ">

  <system.web>

    <pages theme="Smoke" />

  </system.web>

</configuration>
```

Figure 11-1 and Figure 11-2 show a page from the Contoso Magic site as it looks using two different themes. Skin files modify the appearance of the form fields and CSS files modify all the other elements. To view the content of these files, open them in the sample site that comes with this book.

MORE INFO

If you need help obtaining and installing the sample files for this book, refer to the section titled, "Obtaining and Installing the Sample Files For This Book," in Chapter 1.

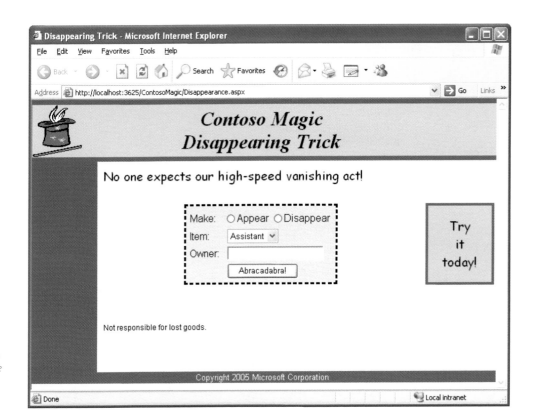

Figure 11-1
This mostly-gray Web page uses a custom theme named **Smoke**. *With no theme in effect, the color scheme would resemble that of Figure 9-5 (in Chapter 9). Note the changes in typography as well.*

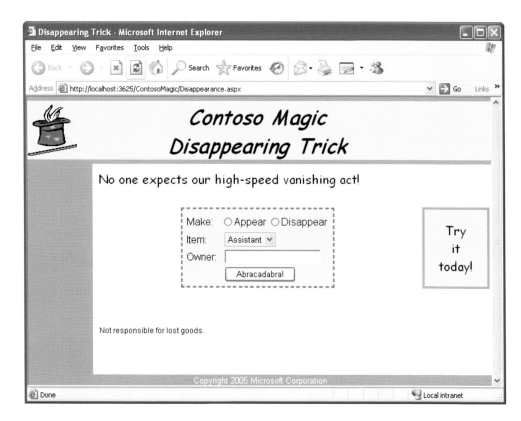

Figure 11-2
Here's the same page with the Mirrors theme in effect. Bright reflected colors are the inspiration.

In Summary...

ASP.NET 2.0 themes can centrally control the appearance of any ASP.NET 2.0 site. Within a theme, skin files control Web server controls and CSS files control ordinary HTML elements.

Skin files contain XML code that you edit by hand. To modify the value of a given server control attribute, you code the same tag and attribute names that appear in the Web page.

To apply a Theme to a specific page, modify the page's Theme attribute. To apply a Theme to an entire Web site, add a <pages theme="*theme-name*" /> tag to the web.config file.

The next chapter will explain how to code a site map and then use it to create dynamic menus, tree view menus, and breadcrumbs.

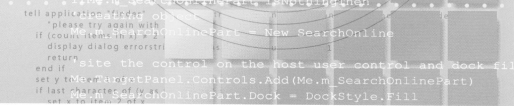

Chapter 12

Linking the Pages in Your Site Automatically

Every Web site needs an orderly collection of hyperlinks that helps visitors find their way to the information they're seeking. In a large site, keeping these links clear, simple, and well-organized can be a daunting task, particularly as developers make changes and apply updates occur over time. To help with this task, ASP.NET 2.0 provides four new components:

- **A Site Map File** that documents the site's logical structure.

- **A *Menu* Control** that reads the site map file and displays drop-down or fly-out dynamic menus.

- **A *TreeView* Control** that reads the site map file and displays an expandable, collapsible, indented list of links.

- **A *SiteMapPath* Control** that searches the site map file for the URL of the current page, and then displays a series of links (breadcrumbs) that lead back to the home page.

Working together, these four components make it very easy to organize your site and display your hyperlinks in the most up-to-date, visually attractive, and compact way. The rest of this chapter will explain how to make this happen on any site you create.

IMPORTANT

The use of ASP.NET 2.0 navigation controls is entirely optional. If you prefer, you can create your site structure, hyperlinks, and menus manually or with a compatible third-party tool.

Creating a Site Map for Your Web Site

All three ASP.NET 2.0 navigation controls have so many options and so much flexibility that new developers sometimes have trouble finding a starting point. The solution, in most cases, is to first create a site map file. The procedure for doing this should be quite familiar.

TO CREATE A SITE MAP FILE

1 Open the site you want to map, then choose **New File** from the File menu.

2 When the New Item dialog box appears, select the **Site Map** template.

3 If this is the first site map in your site, accept the default filename. Otherwise, override the suggested filename base.

4 Click the **Add** button.

By default, this procedure creates a file named Web.sitemap located in the site's root folder. The default name and location are both good choices. In fact, you shouldn't change the file name.

Internally, ASP.NET 2.0 site maps are XML files. Microsoft Visual Web Developer™ therefore displays them in text mode. Omitting comments and abbreviating the *xmlns* attribute (which is constant), a new site map file looks like this:

```
1    <?xml version="1.0" encoding="utf-8" ?>
2    <siteMap xmlns="... " >
3        <siteMapNode url="" title="" description="">
4            <siteMapNode url="" title="" description="" />
5            <siteMapNode url="" title="" description="" />
6        </siteMapNode>
7    </siteMap>
```

The format of this file is relatively straightforward.

- The <?xml> tag on line 1 identifies the version of XML in use. Don't modify this tag.

- The <siteMap> tag on line 2 and its closing </siteMap> tag on line 7 mark the beginning and end of the XML document. Don't modify these tags either.

- Every <siteMap> tag must contain one and only one top-level <siteMapNode> tag. This defines the starting page in the site map—usually the site's Home page. In the example, this is the tag on line 3. Its closing tag is on line 6.

- Between the top-level <siteMapNode> tag and its closing tag, you can add as many additional <siteMapNode> tags as you like. Each of these tags will become "level two" nodes in your drop-down menu or expandable tree view. Lines 4 and 5 provide examples.

- Within each level two <siteMapNode> tag you can add as many level three <siteMapNode> tags as you like, and so forth.

TIP

Remember that the forms:
and
are equivalent, except that the second form can enclose additional tags.

This is actually a simple process. Just visualize how you want visitors to navigate through your site, then indent (or *nest*) a set of <siteMapNode> tags the same way. For example, if you want this logical structure:

```
Home Page
        Products
                Cloaks
                Rubber Daggers
        Services
                Dry Cleaning
                Vulcanizing
```

code your <siteMapNode> tags like this:

```
<siteMapNode url="default.aspx"  title="Home Page">

  <siteMapNode url="products.aspx"  title="Products">

    <siteMapNode url="cloaks.aspx"    title="Cloaks" />

    <siteMapNode url="daggers.aspx"  title="Rubber Daggers" />

  </siteMapNode>

  <siteMapNode url="services.aspx" title="Services">

    <siteMapNode url="dryclean.aspx" title="Dry Cleaning" />

    <siteMapNode url="vulcaniz.aspx" title="Vulcanizing" />

  </siteMapNode>

</siteMapNode>
```

There are only three <siteMapNode> attributes to consider for now. They are:

- **URL** The absolute or relative location of the page. This is where the link in your menu or tree view will direct a visitor, or where the reverse path of breadcrumbs will begin.

  Don't specify the same URL value twice in the same site map file. Otherwise, an error will occur whenever you browse a page that contains a *Menu*, *TreeView*, or *SiteMapPath* (breadcrumb) control.

  For relative locations, it's best to code a tilde and slash (~/) followed by the path from the application root. Here are two examples:

  ```
  url="~/default.aspx"
  url="~/products/wands.aspx"
  ```

  SEE ALSO

  Chapter 17 will describe a *role=* attribute you can add to any <siteMapNode> tag. Combined with other techniques, this attribute hides menu items that the current visitor lacks permission to access.

  To create a <siteMapNode> that doesn't link to another page, leave its URL value blank. This is useful for menu items that group deeper target pages, but have no target pages themselves.

- **title** The name of the page in natural language, such as Home Page or Contact Us. This will appear as the visible text in your menu, tree view, or breadcrumb.

- **description** A longer description. This will appear as tool tip text when the mouse is over the link. This field is optional.

Figure 12-1 shows how Visual Web Developer displays the site map file for the Contoso Magic site. Figure 12-2 shows a fly-out menu based on this site map. The next section will explain how to create such a menu.

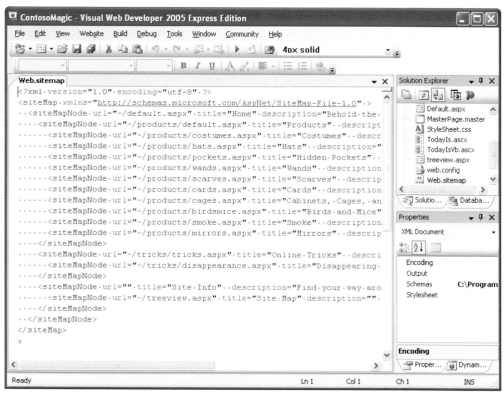

Figure 12-1
This is how Visual Web Developer displays the site map file for the Contoso Magic Web site.

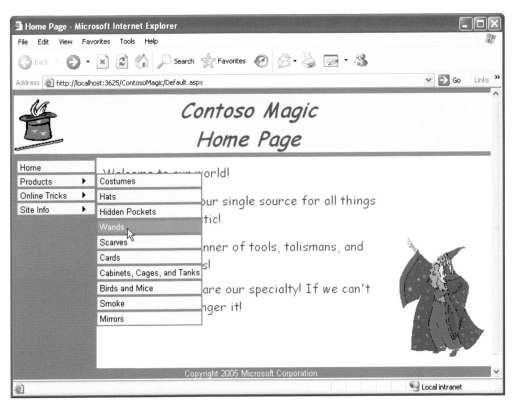

Figure 12-2
The Menu control in this page derives
its structure from the site map shown
in Figure 12-1.

Creating Drop-Down and Fly-Out Menus

You can add drop-down or fly-out menus to master pages, Web user controls, or individual pages.

TO CREATE A DROP-DOWN OR FLY-OUT MENU

1 Open the master page, Web user control, or page that will display the menu.

2 In the Toolbox, open the **Data** group and drag a **SiteMapDataSource** control onto the open page. You can put this control anywhere you want, but keep it out of the way. It won't display anything when a Web visitor browses the page.

Visual Web Developer will assign a name such as *SiteMapDS* or *SiteMapDS1* to this control. As shown below, this name appears on the face of the control. You'll need this control name in step 4.

> SiteMapDataSource - SiteMapDS

3 In the Toolbox, open the **Navigation** group and drag a **Menu** control onto the open page. Drop it wherever you want the menu to appear.

4 Visual Web Developer will display a task menu like the one shown in Figure 12-3. Open the **Choose Data Source** drop-down list and specify the name of the SiteMapDataSource control you added in step 2.

5 Save the page, then right-click it and choose **Preview In Browser**.

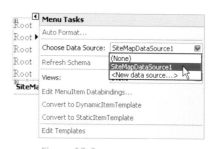

Figure 12-3
A Menu control's task menu specifies, among other things, where the menu should get its list of links.

To further configure the menu, select it and then specify any values you want in the Properties window. The Orientation setting, for example, selects between:

- **Horizontal** Top-level menu items will appear left to right. The result is a drop-down menu system.

- **Vertical** Top-level menu items will appear top to bottom. This creates a fly-out menu system.

NOTE

A static menu item is one that's always visible. Dynamic menu items appear only when you select their parent in the menu tree.

Table 12-1 shows the non-default settings in effect for the menu shown previously in Figure 12-2.

Setting	Value	Description
DataSourceID	SiteMapDS	Tells the menu to get its links from the site map file that the SiteMapDataSource control named SiteMapDS specifies.
StaticDisplayLevels	2	Tells the menu to display the first two menu levels at all times. The remaining levels will appear dynamically (that is, only when selected).
StaticSubMenuIndent	(empty)	Tells the menu not to indent level two menu items any more than it indents level one items (i.e. the Home page).
StaticMenuItemStyle-CssClass	MenuStaItm	Specifies a CSS rule that controls the default appearance of static menu items.
StaticHoverStyle-CssClass	MenuStaHov	Specifies a CSS rule that controls the appearance of static menu items when the mouse is over them.
DynamicMenuItemStyle-CssClass	MenuDynItm	Specifies a CSS rule that controls the default appearance of dynamic menu items.
DynamicHoverStyle-CssClass	MenuDynHov	Specifies a CSS rule that controls the appearance of dynamic menu items when the mouse is over them.

Table 12-1
Menu Properties in Effect for Figure 12-2

There's nothing special about these seven properties or their values; yours will be different, depending on the requirements of your site. Nevertheless, these seven illustrate some typical choices.

Specifying CSS rules for the various types of menu items follows the practice of centralizing all font and color decisions in CSS style sheets. To finish this task you must, of course, define the matching style rules.

If your menu structure becomes too large or too complex, you might choose to use several site map files instead of one. For example, you might create three separate site map files: for Products; for Services; and for the Home page and all other pages. Within each of these areas, you would then point any *SiteMapDataSource* controls (and hence *Menu* controls) to the appropriate site map file.

The <asp:menu> control is incredibly flexible. For example:

- If you choose Data Source: None on the control's task menu, you can click the nearby Edit Menu Items link and configure a set of menu links manually.

- If you choose a data source other than a SiteMapDataSource, you can generate menus on the fly based on records in a database. To map database fields to menu items, configure the Menu control's *DataBindings* property.

- You can easily configure the colors, fonts, icon files, and other visual properties of each type of menu item.

- If you change a site's theme, any Menu controls the site contains will change their appearance based on the skin files and CSS files in that theme.

- By using master pages and Web user controls, you can define a menu once and use it on as many pages as you like.

Creating Tree View Menus

ASP.NET 2.0 can also display the contents of a site map as an expandable, collapsible, indented list. Figure 12-4 provides an example. Web visitors can use the Plus (+) and Minus (-) icons to expand and collapse any nodes they want.

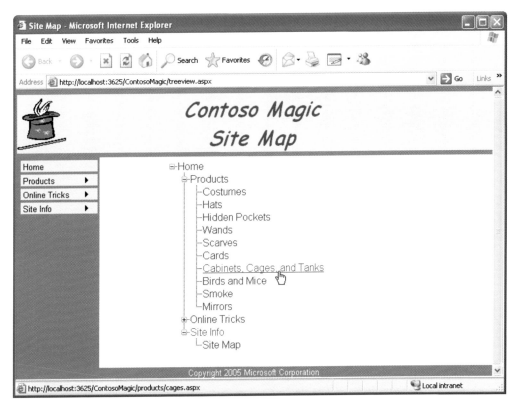

Figure 12-4
A TreeView *control displays the graphical list
of links that appears in the center of this Web
page. The same site map file controls the tree
view and the menu at the left.*

The component that creates
displays like this is an ASP.NET 2.0
TreeView control. The procedure
for adding a *TreeView* control to
a page is almost the same as that
for adding a *Menu* control. The
difference: You drag a *TreeView*
control out of the toolbox rather
than dragging a *Menu* control.

Providing Breadcrumbs

Menu and *TreeView* controls are great for drilling *into* the content of a site, but what about
backtracking or drilling *out* of a site? To support backtracking, many sites provide *breadcrumbs*, a list of links that leads, step by step, from the current page back to the Home page.

Manually coding and updating breadcrumb on each page is so tedious and-error prone
that few Web developers attempt it. Fortunately, a new *SiteMapPath* control included with
ASP.NET 2.0 makes this task easy. This control finds the current page in your site map and
reads backward to the Home page, creating links at each level.

In Figure 12-5, for example, a *SiteMapPath* control appears in the top left corner of the main content area. The *SiteMapPath* control displays Home > Online Tricks > Disappearing Trick based on data in the site's Web.sitemap file. The menu at the left uses the same site map file and therefore displays the same links.

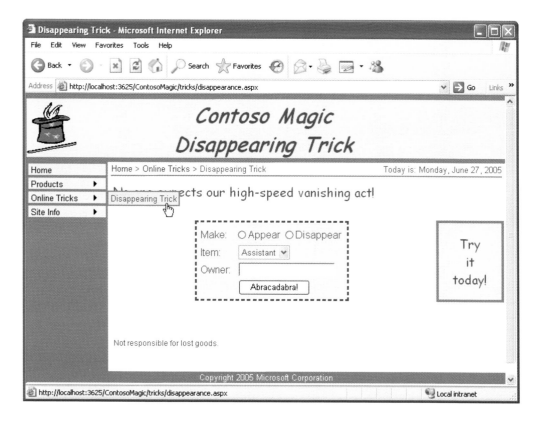

Figure 12-5.
A single **SiteMapPath** *control displays the breadcrumbs that appear just below the banner of this Web page. The* **SiteMapPath** *control and the menu at the left both use the same site map file. The* **TodayIs** *control from Chapter 8 displays the current date.*

You can add a *SiteMapPath* control to any .aspx Web page, any master page, or any Web user control. In the Toolbox, open the Navigation group and then drag a *SiteMapPath* control into Design view.

Unlike the *Menu* and *TreeView* controls, a *SiteMapPath* control doesn't get its data from a *SiteMapDataSource*. Unless your server administrator has made special arrangements, a *SiteMapPath* control always uses the default site map file, Web.sitemap. This is a good reason not to override the default filename when you create the primary (or only) site map file for your site

In Summary...

ASP.NET 2.0 provides four server controls that help you organize and implement hyperlinks within your site. The first, a *SiteMapDataSource* control, provides access to a hierarchical list of links you code in an XML file named, by default, web.sitemap. This control displays nothing to the Web visitor, but it provides data to the *Menu* and *TreeView* controls.

The *Menu* control displays a system of drop-down or fly-out menus based on data that the *SiteMapDataSource* control provides. The *TreeView* control displays the same data as a hierarchical, expandable, and collapsible list of links. To add either of these controls to a Web page, master page, or user control, first add a *SiteMapDataSource* control, then add the *Menu* or *TreeView* control and configure it to use the *SiteMapDataSource* control.

The fourth control, *SiteMapPath*, finds the current page in the site's web.sitemap file, then displays each link between the current page and the site's home page. This provides a breadcrumb or backtracking facility.

The next chapter explains how to use Visual Web Developer for creating databases and connecting Web sites to them.

Chapter 13

Creating and Connecting to Databases

Used together, databases and the World Wide Web exceed the sum of their parts. Without this combination, none of today's most popular and most useful Web sites would be possible. There would be no portals, no search engines, no e-commerce, no auctions, no on-line banking, and no on-line travel reservations. The Web would be little more than a pile of electronic brochures.

Microsoft® Visual Web Developer™ makes it very easy to create Web sites that leverage the power of databases. Working with databases is such a simple process that in many cases you won't need to write a single line of program code.

Visual Web Developer includes powerful, integrated, and easy-to-use features for working with Microsoft SQL Server™, Microsoft's premier database management system. The combination of Visual Web Developer 2005 Express and SQL Server 2005 Express is so powerful, simple, and inexpensive that Microsoft recommends SQL Server as the best solution not only for professional developers but also for hobbyists and small Web shops.

This is the first of four chapters explaining the database features of Visual Web Developer. All four chapters assume you've installed SQL Server Express on the same machine as Visual Web Developer. If you haven't done so already, it's time to install SQL Server Express.

> **NOTE**
> Throughout this chapter and the next three, unless otherwise stated, the term *SQL Server* refers to Microsoft SQL Server 2000, SQL Server 2005, or SQL Server 2005 Express Edition.

Administering Data Access

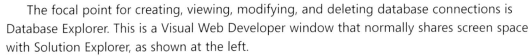

To use a database with Visual Web Developer, you must first configure a *data connection* that points to the specific database you want.

Each data connection points to one— and only one—database. This isn't a limitation because:

■ You can configure as many data connections as you need.

■ Each Web site can use as many data connections as you need.

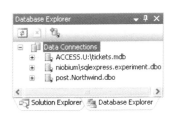

The focal point for creating, viewing, modifying, and deleting database connections is Database Explorer. This is a Visual Web Developer window that normally shares screen space with Solution Explorer, as shown at the left.

To switch between Solution Explorer and Database Explorer, click one of the tabs at the bottom of the window. If neither the Database Explorer window nor the Database Explorer tab is visible, choose Database Explorer from the View menu.

The next section explains how to create a data connection for an existing database. The section after that explains how to create both a new database and a new data connection that points to the database.

Connecting to an Existing Database

Here's the procedure for connecting to any type of database that your version of Microsoft Visual Studio® supports.

TO CONNECT TO A DATABASE

1 Start Visual Web Developer and display the Database Explorer window. Don't bother opening or closing any particular Web site.

2 In Database Explorer, right-click the top-level node (titled Data Connections) and choose **Add Connection** from the shortcut menu.

3 If a Choose Data Source or Change Data Source dialog box like the one shown in Figure 13-1 appears, review the entries in the Data Source list box and select the one that describes your database.

If multiple providers (or drivers) are available for the type of database you choose, the Data Provider drop-down list will display them. In general, .NET data providers are the most reliable, most secure, and best performing.

To change the default data provider for a given type of database, first select a data source, then select a data provider, and finally select the **Always Use This Selection** check box.

To save your changes and close the Change Data Source dialog box, click the **OK** button.

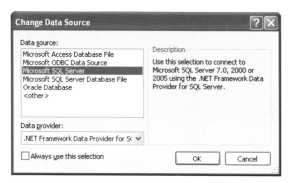

Figure 13-1
Visual Web Developer can connect to many types of databases. However, it provides the most capability with SQL Server databases.

4 When the Add Connection dialog box appears, inspect the box titled Data Source.

■ If the Data Source box refers to the type of database you want, proceed to the next step.

■ Otherwise, click the Change button and revert to step 3.

The appearance of the Add Connection dialog box varies depending on the type of database. In all cases, however, the Data Source field appears in the same place at the top of the dialog box. Figure 13-2 shows how the Add Connection dialog box looks for an existing Microsoft SQL Server database.

5 Configure the Add Connection dialog box as required for the type of database, then click the **OK** button.

Figure 13-2
This dialog box configures a data connection from Visual Web Developer to SQL Server.

TO CONFIGURE THE ADD CONNECTION DIALOG BOX FOR A SQL SERVER DATABASE

1 In the Server Name box, enter the computer name and, if necessary, the instance name where SQL Server is running the database you want.

Note that clicking the Server Name drop-down arrow lists computer names but not instance names. To access a copy of SQL Server Express running on a computer named SPOOKY, you could select the name SPOOKY from the drop-down list, but you'd have to type *\SqlExpress*. The complete server name would be SPOOKY\SqlExpress.

> **NOTE**
>
> An *instance name* identifies a specific copy of SQL Server running on a computer. If two copies of SQL Server are running on the same computer, they must have different instances names such as *clowns* and *acrobats*, *test* and *prod*, or *visible* and *""* (none). SQL Server Express always runs with the instance name *SqlExpress*.

2 Select the type of authentication SQL Server will recognize. The options are:

■ **Use Windows Authentication** Uses your current Microsoft Windows® logon account for connecting to SQL Server. This is usually the correct choice for local copies of SQL Server Express and for full copies of SQL Server that use Windows Authentication.

■ **Use SQL Server Authentication** Uses a SQL Server user name and password for connecting to SQL server. If you select this option, you must also enter the SQL Server user name and password that have the privileges you need. Typically, a database administrator controls these usernames and passwords.

3 Specify which database the connection will use.

If the database is already attached to SQL Server, select the database from the drop-down list titled Select Or Enter A Database Name.

4 If the database is in an .mdf file not yet attached to SQL server:

- Specify the .mdf filename in the Attach A Database File text box. You can either type the path and file-name you want or click the browse button, locate the file, and click the Open button.

- In the Logical Name box, type a brief name that describes the database you're attaching. This name will appear in later drop-down lists, and it's the name you'll use in SQL statements and any program code you write.

5 To check your work, click the Test Connection button in the lower left corner of the dialog box. If your settings are correct, Visual Web Developer will display "Test connection succeeded." If you get a different response, recheck your work.

6 Click the OK button to create the connection.

The new connection should appear immediately in Database Explorer. Here are some ways to see what the database contains:

- Clicking the Plus (+) icon that precedes the new data connection name should display a list of object types that the database contains: tables, views, stored procedures, and other object types.

- Clicking the Plus (+) icon that precedes an object type should display a list of objects of that type. For example, clicking the Plus icon (+) that precedes Tables will display a list of tables.

- Clicking the Plus (+) icon that precedes a table should display a list of fields and so forth..

If you fail to get these results, your database or your database connection are probably incorrect.

Creating a New Database

Physically, SQL Server databases reside in two files: a main file with a filename, extension of .mdf and a log file with an extension of .ldf. These files can reside anywhere on the computer where SQL Server is running, but the following locations are customary.

■ For databases that only one ASP.NET 2.0 Web site will use, the most convenient location is that Web site's App_Data folder. This greatly simplifies publishing the database and getting it to work on the remote site.

■ For databases that multiple applications or Web sites will use, the best location is usually the SQL Server default Data folder. This usually resembles
C:\Program Files\Microsoft SQL Server\MSSQL.1\MSSQL\Data

Regardless of location, you can create new SQL Server databases directly in Visual Web Developer. The rest of this book, for example, will use a SQL Server database named ContosoMagic.mdf that resides in the sample Web site's App_Data folder.

TO CREATE THE SQL SERVER DATABASE FOR THE SAMPLE SITE

1 Open the Web site in Visual Web Developer.

2 Choose **New File** from the File menu.

3 When the Add New Item dialog box appears, select **SQL Database** in the Templates box.

4 In the Name box, type **ContosoMagic.mdf**.

5 Click the **Add** button. If a prompt like the following appears, click the **Yes** button. Visual Web Developer will create the database and the data connection.

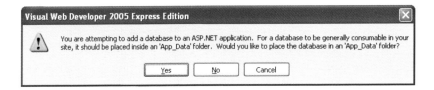

Microsoft Visual Web Developer 2005 Express Edition: Build a Web Site Now!

TO CREATE A DATABASE THAT RESIDES IN SQL SERVER'S DEFAULT DATA FOLDER

1 In Database Explorer, right-click the top-level node (titled Data Connections) and choose **Create New SQL Server Database** from the shortcut menu.

2 When the Create New SQL Server Database dialog box shown in Figure 13-3 appears, specify the database server name just as you did when connecting to an existing database in the previous section. If, for example, you're running SQL Server Express on a computer named NIOBIUM, specify NIOBIUM\SqlExpress.

3 In the Log On To The Server frame, specify your credentials for creating the database. For SQL Server Express, this is usually Windows authentication.

4 In the New Database Name box, type a brief name that describes the database you're creating.

5 Click the **OK** button to create the database. For your convenience, Visual Web Developer will immediately create a data connection as well.

Figure 13-3
This dialog box creates a new SQL Server database and a new data connection to match. It doesn't, however, create any tables.

Adding and Modifying Database Tables

Visual Web Developer can directly create, modify, and delete tables in SQL Server databases. For example, to create a Products table in the ContosoMagic database, proceed as follows.

TO CREATE A PRODUCTS TABLE IN THE CONTOSOMAGIC DATABASE

1 In the Database Explorer window, click the **Plus (+)** icon next to the ContosoMagic data connection you created in the previous section. Then, right-click the **Tables** entry and select **Add New Table** from the shortcut menu.

2 Visual Web Developer will display a Table Designer for naming and describing the fields in your new table. To create the first field, proceed as follows:

a. Set the insertion point in the first row of the Table Designer, under the Column Name field.

b. Enter the name *ProductId* and press the Tab key.

c. In the Data Type column, select Int from the dropdown list and press the Tab key.

d. Clear the check box in the Allow Nulls column.

e. In the Column Properties tab near the bottom of the window, scroll down to Identity Specification, click the Plus (+) icon to expand it, and set the (Is Identity) property to Yes. Figure 13-4 shows this step in progress.

f. Right-click anywhere in the new *ProductId* row and select Set Primary Key from the shortcut menu.

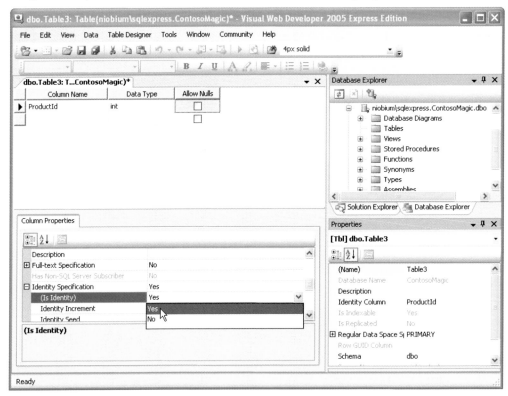

Figure 13-4
Visual Web Developer includes a Table Designer that can add, modify, and delete fields in a database table.

Setting the **(Is Identity) property** to Yes tells SQL Server that every time it adds a record to the table, it should set the given field to a unique value. Selecting one or more fields, right-clicking the selection, and then choosing Set Primary Key from the shortcut menu tells SQL Server to treat those fields as the true identity of each record.

3 Each time you create a field by filling in the blank row at the bottom of the grid, Visual Web Developer creates a new blank row so you can append another field. Following this pattern, set the insertion point in the second, third, and fourth grid rows and assign the corresponding field properties from Table 13-1.

Column Name	DataType	Allow Nulls	Identity	Primary Key
ProductId	int	Cleared	Yes	Yes
CategoryId	int	Cleared	(default)	(default)
ProductName	varchar(255)	Cleared	(default)	(default)
ProductPrice	money	Cleared	(default)	(default)

Table 13-1
Fields in the ContosoMagic Products Table

4 Choose **Save Table*n*** from the File menu, where *n* is a sequential number that Visual Web Developer will assign. When the Choose Name dialog box shown below appears, enter **Products** and then click the **OK** button.

To add, modify, or delete fields in an existing table, right-click the table in Database Explorer and then choose Open Table Definition. This will display the grid shown in Figure 13-4.

To delete a table, right-click it in Database Explorer and choose Delete. This deletes both the table definition and any data the table might contain.

Viewing and Updating Database Table Content

To view the data in any table, right-click the table name in Database Explorer and choose Show Table Data. This starts a part of Visual Web Developer called the Query Developer that queries and displays the data in that table. As shown in Figure 13-5, the Query Designer window contains up to four panes.

Figure 13-5
Initially, the Query Designer displays only the Results pane that appears here at the bottom. The top three panes graphically configure more advanced queries.

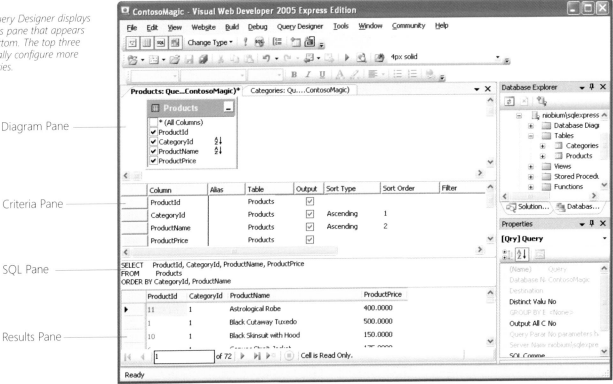

Initially, Query Designer runs a very simple query and displays the results in the Results pane. This is a very simple view that looks somewhat like a spreadsheet. You can use this view to change, add, or delete records:

- To change the value of any field, select it and type the new value.

- To add a record, type its data values into the blank row at the end of the table.

- To delete a record, select it and then press the Del key.

Visual Web Developer immediately inserts, updates, or deletes the current record whenever you press Enter, press Del, or move to another record. There's no need to save anything before you close the view.

If you simply want a quick look at your data, perhaps to make a few corrections, the Results pane may be all you need. If, however, you want to perform more complex queries or just want more control, the other three panes can be very useful. To display any of these panes:

1. Right-click the Query Designer window.

2. Choose Pane from the shortcut menu.

3. Select the pane you want to display or hide.

   Here's a brief description of each pane and some reasons you might want to use it:

- **Diagram** Displays a small window for each table involved in the query. Check boxes indicate fields destined for output, and AZ icons indicate ordering in ascending or descending sequence.

  - To add a table to the diagram (and hence to the query) drag it from Database Explorer and drop it in the Diagram pane.

  - To *join* any pair of tables (that is, to find matching records based on data values) drag the field you want to match from one table and drop it on the field you want to match in the other table.

  - To modify the join properties, right-click the line connecting the two tables and choose the type of join you want.

- **Criteria** Displays a tabular, editable view of the fields and tables involved in the query.

- **SQL Display**s the SQL statement that generates the query.

Whenever you update the Diagram, Criteria, or SQL pane, Visual Web Developer will update the other two panes. If, for example, you modify the SQL pane, Visual Web Developer will update the Diagram and Criteria panes accordingly.

■ **Results** Displays the results of running the query. The default query that appears when you first choose the Show Table Data command is:

```
SELECT * FROM <table-name>
```

where <table-name> is the name of your table.

If you use the Diagram, Criteria, or SQL pane to change this query, the Results pane won't show the effects until you either:

■ Choose Execute SQL from the Query Designer menu, or

■ Right-click the Query Designer window and choose Execute SQL from the shortcut menu.

In Summary...

Visual Web Developer can connect your Web site to as many existing databases as you like. It can also create databases and connect to them in one operation. These databases typically reside in your Web site's App_Data folder or in SQL Server's default Data folder.

Visual Web Developer can also create, modify, and update database tables and records, all without forcing you to leave the program.

The next chapter will explain how to create a simple Web page that updates the Products table you created in this chapter.

Chapter 14

Displaying Database Information

Database programming has a reputation for being a difficult task, and with good reason. Databases are both complex and mission-critical. Databases are also so important and so useful, however, that software makers are continually striving to provide intuitive and easy-to-use database tools. Microsoft® ASP.NET 2.0 and Microsoft Visual Web Developer™ provide some of the best and most user-friendly tools yet.

With Visual Web Developer, you can create simple- to moderately-complex Web database applications using only the graphical design interface. This involves three kinds of components:

- **Data Connections** Provide pathways to databases. Chapter 13 explained how to create and modify these pathways.

- **Data Sources** Work through data connections to retrieve, insert, update, and delete database records, but display nothing to the Web visitor.

- **Data-Bound Controls** Retrieve and display information from a data source. In the case of insert, update, and delete operations, data-bound controls also supply the data source with information for processing.

This chapter explains how to use and create data sources and how to use data-bound controls for displaying data. Chapter 15 will explain how to use these controls for making database changes.

Using Data Sources

To appreciate the power of data sources and data-bound controls, try this simple procedure:

1. In Database Explorer, expand any existing data connection and locate a table or query you'd like to display in a Web page.

2. Open the Web page in Design view.

3. Drag the table or query out of Database Explorer and drop it onto the open page.

As shown in Figure 14-1, this adds two controls to the Web page: a data source control (in this case, a *SqlDataSource* control named *SqlDataSource1*) and a *GridView* control (which displays the tabular grid with the database fields as column headings.) The *GridView* is one of the most popular and most useful data-bound controls. Visual Web Developer automatically *binds* (that is, connects) the new *GridView* to the new data source.

You can also create a data source by dragging an icon out of the Toolbox's Data group and dropping it onto your page. Table 14-1 describes some of the most popular data source controls. The Toolbox in your copy of Visual Web Developer might offer more or fewer data source controls, depending on its version and on other software you've installed.

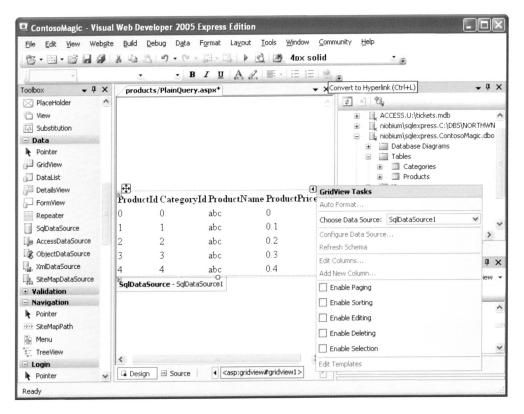

Figure 14-1
Dragging a table or query from Database Explorer to an open Web page creates two controls: a data source control and a GridView control. It also displays the GridView control's task menu.

Table 14-1
Common ASP.NET 2.0 Data Source
Controls

Control	Description
SqlDataSource	Retrieves and updates information in Microsoft SQL Server™ databases.
AccessDataSource	Retrieves and updates information in Microsoft Access databases.
ObjectDataSource	Retrieves and updates information through a custom object. In an application with three tiers (presentation, business logic, and data access) the bound control would typically be in the presentation tier and the custom object would be in the business logic tier.
XmlDataSource	Retrieves and optionally transforms information in XML files.
SiteMapDataSource	Retrieves information from an XML site map file. Chapter 12 explained how to use a site map file and a SiteMapDataSource control to display hyperlinks in Menu, TreeView, and SiteMapPath controls.

Configuring Data Sources

When you create a data source by dragging a table or query from Database Explorer, it delivers all the records and all the fields in that table or query, without sorting. To change these defaults or to configure a data source you created from the Toolbox, proceed as follows.

TO CONFIGURE A DATA SOURCE

1 Select the data source control, click its smart tag icon, and select **Configure Data Source** from the resulting task menu.

2 When the Choose Your Data Connection dialog box shown in Figure 14-2 appears, either:

■ Use the drop-down box to select the data connection you want, or

■ Click the New Connection button to create a new data connection. This displays the Add Connection dialog box that Chapter 13 explained.

To display the connection string the data source will use, click the Plus (+) icon that precedes the Connection String setting

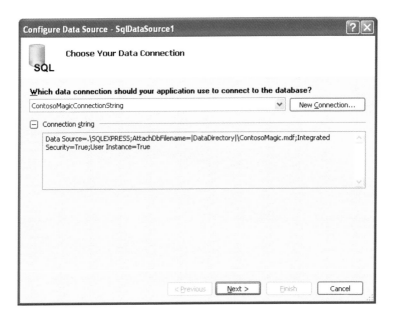

3 Click the **Next** button to display the Configure The Select Statement dialog box shown in Figure 14-3. For simple queries, select **Specify Columns From A Table Or View** and configure these settings:

■ **Name** Select the table or query you want. The drop-down choices will all come from the data connection you specified on the first page of the wizard.

■ **Columns** Select the check box that precedes each field you want the data source to retrieve or update. To specify all the fields, select the asterisk (*) check box.

■ **Return Only Unique Rows** Select this check box if, when two or more records have identical data values, you only want to retrieve one of them.

- **WHERE** Click this button to display an Add WHERE Clause dialog box. This provides a means to return only those records having certain data values. For example, you can specify that the value of a given field must match the value of a constant, another control on the Web page, a cookie, a conventional HTML form field, an ASP.NET profile field, a query string variable, or a session variable.

- **ORDER BY** Click this button to display an Add ORDER BY Clause dialog box where you can specify one, two, or three fields to use in sorting the data.

- **Advanced** Click this button to display an Advanced SQL Generation Options dialog box. If you plan to use the data source for updating, select the check box titled Generate INSERT, UPDATE, And DELETE Statements. The other option on this dialog box, Use Optimistic Concurrency, is a tuning factor you might need to adjust in very busy environments.

If these options don't provide the flexibility you need, ignore them and select **Specify A Custom SQL Statement Or Stored Procedure** near the top of the dialog box.

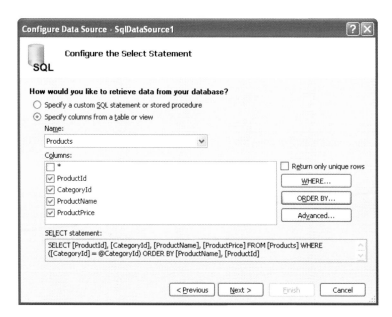

Figure 14-3
This wizard page specifies which fields and records the data source should provide, and in what order.

4 If you selected Specify A Custom SQL Statement Or Stored Procedure in the previous step, clicking the **Next** button will display the Define Custom Statements Or Stored Procedures dialog box shown in Figure 14-4.

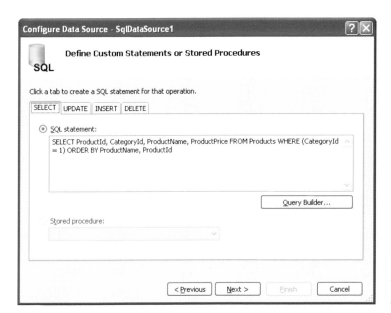

Figure 14-4
If you choose to use a custom SQL statement or stored procedure, the wizard displays this page so you can supply those statements.

To specify a custom SELECT, UPDATE, INSERT, or DELETE statement, select the corresponding tab and then click the **Query Builder** button. This displays the same query designer that Chapter 13 described in the section titled *Viewing and Updating Database Table Contents*. Develop your SQL statement, test it by clicking the **Execute Query** button, then click the **OK** button.

5 Clicking the **Next** button displays the last page in the wizard, the Test Query dialog box shown in Figure 14-5. Click the **Test Query** button and verify that the central box displays the data you want. If it's correct, click the **Finish** button. If not, click the **Previous** button and modify your entries.

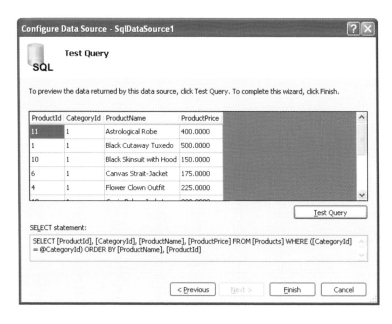

Figure 14-5
When you click the Test Query button in this dialog box, the wizard displays a preview of what the data source will deliver.

Note that each data source control stores only one configuration: that is, one table or query, one selection of fields, one sort order, and so forth. If your page needs to access two or more tables—or the same table or query with different criteria—you'll need to add and configure a separate data source control for each one.

Displaying Database Information

Many ASP.NET 2.0 Web server controls can bind to a data source. For example, to fill a drop-down list with choices from a database table, set these three properties on any *DropDownList* control:

- **DataSourceID** The name of a data source control that points to the table or query that provides the data.

- **DataTextField** The name of the field that provides the values the Web visitor will see. This is usually a text field such as *ProductName* or *CategoryName*.

- **DataValueField** The name of the field that provides the values the Web page will submit. This is often a code field such as *ProductId* or *CategoryId*.

In many case, however, developers want to display multiple fields or even multiple records in a single control, and perhaps support database updating as well. To handle such requirements, ASP.NET 2.0 provides the controls listed in Table 14-2.

Table 14-2
Bound Data Display Controls

Control	Description	Supports Updating	Introduced in ASP.NET
GridView	Displays multiple records in a row and column format.	Update, Delete	2.0
DetailsView	Displays one record at a time using simple HTML.	Insert, Update, Delete	2.0
FormView	Displays one record at a time in a highly formatted form.	Insert, Update, Delete	2.0
DataList	Repeats a custom-designed template once for each record in a data source, merging values from the current record.	Custom Programming	1.0
Repeater	Similar to the *DataList*, but supplies no HTML of its own. This improves flexibility but requires more complex templates.	Custom Programming	1.0

Of these five controls, the *GridView*, *DetailsView*, and *FormView* are the newest, the easiest to use, and therefore the most interesting. The configuration process is essentially the same for each of them.

The remainder of this chapter will explain how to configure a *GridView* control to display products for the Contoso Magic site. The next chapter, which explains updating, has an example that uses the *DetailsView* control.

Configuring a *GridView* Control

This section explains how to create the Contoso Magic Costumes page shown in Figure 14-6. The banner, menu, footer, and breadcrumb areas should be familiar, as should the theme; they all come from earlier chapters in this book.

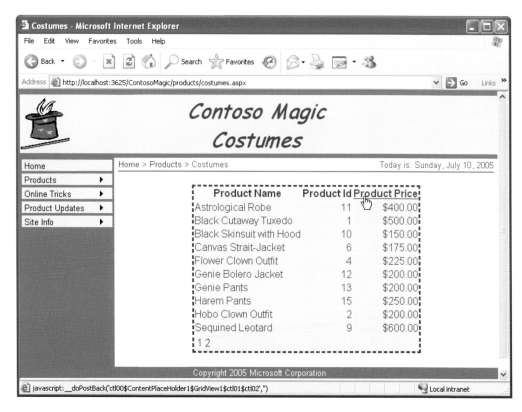

Figure 14-6
A GridView control created the data display in the center of this Web page.

Note the grid displaying the first 10 products in the Costumes category. This is a *GridView* control displaying information from the Products table you created in Chapter 13.

TO CREATE A GRIDVIEW WEB PAGE

1 Open a new blank page, applying any master pages or other formatting you want.

2 Add a *GridView* control and a *SqlDataSource* control to the page. Either:

■ Drag the *Products* table from Database Explorer and drop it onto your page.

■ Drag a *GridView* control and a *SqlDataSource* control from the Data group in the Toolbox, dropping both onto the open Web page.

3 Display the *SqlDataSource* control's task menu and click **Configure Data Source**.

4 When the Choose Your Data Connection dialog box appears, select or create a connection to the ContosoMagic database and then click the Next button.

5 When the Configure The Select Statement dialog box appears, select the Products table and only the *ProductId*, *ProductName*, and *ProductPrice* fields.

6 Click the WHERE button and then, when the Add WHERE Clause dialog box appears, specify these values:

■ **Column** CategoryId

■ **Operator** = (equals)

■ **Source** None

■ **Value** 1 (Note: This setting is in the Parameter Properties frame.)

and then click the **Add** button. This limits the query so that it only returns records having a *CategoryId* number of 1. Figure 14-7 illustrates this configuration.

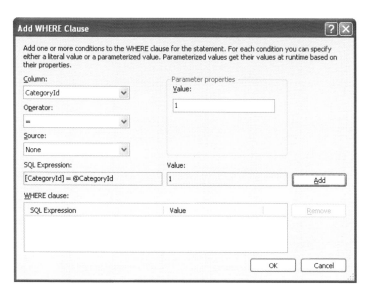

Figure 14-7
This dialog box configures the filter settings for a data source. Don't forget to click the Add button before clicking the OK button.

7 Click the **OK** button to close the Add WHERE Clause dialog box, then click the **Order By** button in the Configure The Select Statement dialog box.

8 When the Add ORDER BY Clause dialog box appears, set Sort By to *ProductName* and then click the **OK** button. This establishes the default sort order for your display.

9 Click the **Next** button, the **Test Query** button, and the **Finish** button to complete the wizard.

Configuring the *GridView* control is a separate operation. To complete this task, proceed as follows.

TO CONFIGURE THE *GRIDVIEW* CONTROL

1 Display the GridView control's task menu and make sure the Choose Data Source drop-down list points to the data source you just configured.

2 Select the following checkboxes:

■ **Enable Paging** Displays only a set number of records at a time. To move between sets, the Web visitor clicks a number at the bottom of the display. The display in Figure 14-6 has two sets of records, numbered 1 and 2.

■ **Enable Sorting** Allows site visitors to sort the display on any column by clicking its heading. In Figure 14-6, the visitor is about to sort the display on Product Price.

3 Click **Edit Columns** in the task menu and then, when the Fields dialog box shown in Figure 14-8 appears, use the Selected Fields box and its accompanying up-arrow and down-arrow buttons to arrange the output fields in this order: *ProductName, ProductId, ProductPrice.*

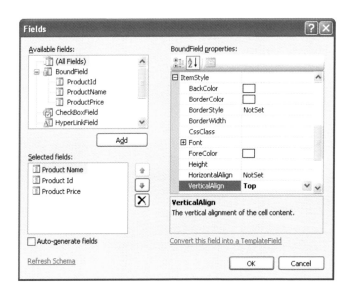

Figure 14-8
With this dialog box you configure which fields a GridView, DetailsView, or FormView control will display, and also how the fields will appear.

4 Select *ProductName* in the Selected Fields box, and then use the BoundField Properties box to apply the properties listed in Table 14-3. Repeat this procedure for the *ProductId*, and *ProductPrice* fields.

Property	Data Field		
DataField	ProductName	ProductId	ProductPrice
DataFormatString			{0:$#,##0.00}
HeaderText	Product Name	Product Id	Product Price
HtmlEncode	True	True	False
Item Style: HorizontalAlign		Right	Right
Item:Style VerticalAlign	Top	Top	Top

Table 14-3
BoundField Properties for the
Costumes.aspx Page

5 Click the **OK** button to close the Fields dialog box, then select the *GridView* and use Visual Web Developer's normal Properties window to configure the following settings. Both of these settings are entirely cosmetic.

■ **CssClass** *formbox* (This is the name of a CSS style rule.)

■ **HorizontalAlign** Center

6 Save the page; then display it in your browser. Test and refine the page, if desired.

The sample Contoso Magic site has a separate page for each of the 10 categories. One is the Costumes page; the other nine are direct copies with only the page title and selection criteria changed. This provides enough pages to make the menu example somewhat realistic.

In a real site, you might prefer a single products page with a drop-down list to select the category. The ConjureCats.aspx page in the sample files provides an example of this technique. This page differs from the Costumes page in that:

■ It contains two *SqlDataSource* controls: one for the Products table and one for a Categories table.

■ It contains a *DropDownList* control configured as the earlier section titled, "Displaying Database Information," explained.

In addition, this control's *AutoPostBack* property is set to True so that changing the selection automatically submits the form and retrieves a list of products in the newly-selected category.

ASP.NET Data Format Strings

The Contoso Magic Costumes page in this section uses the data format string {0:$#,##0.00} to display prices. This is a typical ASP.NET formatting string.

■ A pair of curly braces ({ }) are required delimiters.

■ The colon (:) separates the field number from the format specification.

■ The field number will always be 0, indicating field number one.

■ $#,##0.00 is the actual format. It specifies a leading dollar sign; commas every three digits; zero-suppression except for the ones, tenths, and hundredths positions; and a period as the decimal point.

Continued on next page

Continued from page162

ASP.NET can also format dates and times. For example, {0:dd-MMM-yyyy} would display Harry Houdini's birthday as 24-Mar-1874.

When you specify a custom data format string, you must also specify HtmlEncode=False.

For more information, look up Format Specifiers in the Visual Web Developer Help index.

Displaying Complex Page Elements

By default, the GridView, DetailsView, and FormView controls display all information as plain text. To display information as a check box, hyperlink, picture, or other HTML element:

1. Configure the control as usual until you get to the Fields dialog box shown in Figure 14-8.

Continued on next page

■ In the *SqlDataSource* control for the Products table, the Add WHERE Clause dialog box specifies Control in the Source drop-down list, and *DropDownList1* in the Control ID drop-down list. (The Control ID drop-down list is in the Parameter Properties frame).

The sample files also include a SeekProducts.aspx page where visitors can type a partial product description into a text box, click a Summon button, and receive a list of matching products. This page also resembles the Costumes.aspx page, except that it includes:

■ A *TextBox* control named *txtRune*.

■ A *Button* control named *btnSummon* that submits the form.

■ The following condition in the Add WHERE Clause dialog box of its *SqlDataSource* control:

   ■ **Column** ProductName

   ■ **Operator** LIKE

   ■ **Source** Control

   ■ **ControlID** txtRune

■ A *DataTextField* property that specifies which field supplies the visible text.

■ A *NavigateURL* property that specifies which field supplies the target URL.

In Summary...

Visual Web Developer can create attractive pages that display database information in a variety of ways. To do this without writing any program code requires three components: a data connection that provides a pathway to the database, a data source that retrieves records from the data connection, and finally a data-bound control (often a *GridView*, *DetailsView*, or *FormView* control) that converts the data to HTML for display.

The next chapter will explain how this same collection of controls can update information in databases.

Continued from page 163

2. *In the Available Fields box, select the type of output control you want, then click the Add button. This will add an entry to the Selected Fields box.*

3. *With this new entry selected, configure at least the DataField and HeaderText properties (or their equivalents) in the BoundField Properties box at the right.*

   As you do this, you should be prepared for some variation among output controls. A hyperlink field, for example, has no DataField property. Instead, it has:

   A dataTextField property that specifies which field supplies the visible text.

   A navigateURL property that specifies which field supplies the target URL.

Chapter 15

Maintaining Database Information

Retrieving, organizing, and displaying valuable information is usually a rewarding experience. You enter a little data and get a lot of information back. However, the preliminary step of adding records to a database is less fun. You enter a lot of data and receive few short-term rewards. Nevertheless, someone has to enter the data your site requires. This chapter explains how you can use the *GridView* control from the previous chapter to update or delete records, and how you can use the *DetailsView* control to add records. The chapter also mentions some additional functions that these controls provide. Best of all, none of these techniques requires writing any code.

Using a *GridView* Control to Update and Delete Records

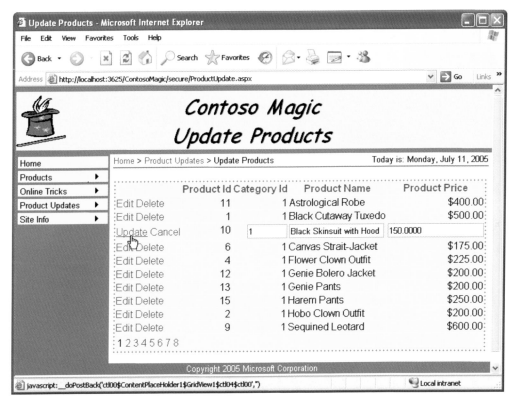

Figure 15-1
When using a GridView control to update a database, the visitor first clicks Edit, overtypes the form fields, and then clicks the Update link.

Figure 15-1 illustrates the *GridView* approach to updating records. For each record, the grid displays any combination you want of these special links.

- **Edit** Uses an HTML form field to display each updatable field a record contains. The Web visitor modifies these values as necessary, then clicks an Update link to save the changes or a Cancel link to abandon them. The figure shows this in progress.

- **Delete** Immediately deletes the corresponding record. There's no, "Are you sure?" prompt.

- **Select** Marks the corresponding record as current. The page in the figure doesn't use this option. For more information about the way this option works, refer to the accompanying sidebar titled, "Double Binding: Not an Escape Trick."

TO CONFIGURE A *GRIDVIEW* CONTROL TO PERFORM UPDATES

1 Make sure that the database table has a primary key. For example, right-click the table in Database Explorer, choose Open Table Definition, and make sure that the field (or each of the fields, if there's more than one) that uniquely identifies each record has a key icon as shown below.

A key icon indicates fields in the primary key.

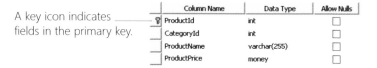

	Column Name	Data Type	Allow Nulls
🔑	ProductId	int	☐
	CategoryId	int	☐
	ProductName	varchar(255)	☐
	ProductPrice	money	☐

If they don't, select the field (or fields) that should serve as the primary key, right-click the selection, and then choose **Set Primary Key** from the shortcut menu.

2 Configure the data source and the *GridView* control so they display the records and fields you want. Browse the page to make sure the display function is working properly.

3 Make sure the data source is configured with INSERT, UPDATE, and DELETE statements. To check this:

■ Select Configure Data Source from the control's task menu.

■ Click the Next button to display the Configure The Select Statement dialog box.

■ If the Advanced button is enabled, click it. When the Advanced SQL Generation Options dialog box appears, make sure the Generate INSERT, UPDATE, And DELETE Statements check box is selected as shown in Figure 15-2.

If either the Advanced button or the Generate INSERT, UPDATE, And DELETE Statements check box is dimmed, and if the check box isn't selected, then close the Advanced SQL Generation Options dialog box (it it's open) and take either of these actions in the Configure The Select Statement dialog box:

Figure 15-2
If you plan to use a data source for updating, you must select the first check box in this dialog box.

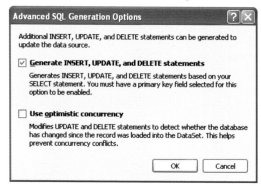

■ With the Specify A Custom SQL Statement Or Stored Procedure option selected, click the Next button to display the Define Custom Statements Or Stored Procedures dialog box. Then, make sure that the UPDATE, INSERT, and DELETE tabs all display valid SQL statements.

■ Select the Specify Columns From A Table Or View option, reconfigure the SELECT statement from scratch, then click the Advanced button and select the Generate INSERT, UPDATE, And DELETE Statements checkbox. (For help reconfiguring the SELECT statement, refer to Chapter 14.)

4 If you're recreating the sample site, create a new ASP.NET Web page in a folder named secure/, name it UpdateProducts.aspx, and add *SqlDataSource* and *GridView* controls as you did in the previous chapter.

5 Display the *GridView* control's task menu and select any combination of these check boxes:

■ **Enable Editing** Select this check box if you want the *GridView* control to modify existing database records.

■ **Enable Deleting** Select this check box if you want the *GridView* control to delete existing database records.

■ **Enable Selection** Select this check box if you want the *GridView* control to designate records as current. Field values from that record will then appear in any other controls bound to the same data source.

6 Save the page, view it in a browser, and test.

The sample files for the ContosoMagic site include a ProductUpdate.aspx page that illustrates these techniques. This page resides in a subfolder named /secure/. Chapter 17 will explain how to stop unauthorized visitors from using pages in that folder.

Using a *DetailsView* Control to Add Records

Using a *GridView* control to update or delete records is simple and intuitive. Using a *GridView* control to add records, however, requires writing some fairly complicated program code. To add records without writing any program code at all, you can use a *DetailsView* control.

To create a page that uses a *DetailsView* control for adding records to the Products table in the Contoso Magic database, proceed as follows.

TO CREATE A PAGE THAT USES A *DETAILSVIEW* CONTROL

1 Create a new blank page named ProductAdd.aspx and located in the same /secure/ folder as the ProductUpdate.aspx page from the previous section. Apply any master pages or other formatting you want.

2 Add a *SqlDataSource* control to the page by dragging it from the Data group in the Toolbox. Configure this data source to access the Products table in the ContosoMagic database.

When you get to the second page of the Wizard, click the **Advanced** button and make sure that the Generate INSERT, UPDATE, And DELETE Statements check box is selected.

3 Add a *DetailsView* control to the page by dragging it from the Toolbox.

4 Configure the following fields on the task menu for the new *DetailsView* control.

■ **Choose Data Source** Select the data source you created in step 2.

■ **Enable Inserting** Select this check box.

5 Switch to the Properties window and make sure the new *DetailsView* control is selected. Then, verify that the property settings in Table 15-1 are in effect.

6 Save the page, view it in a browser, and test. Any records you create should appear the next time you refresh any of the product pages.

NOTE

Like the *DetailsView* control, a *FormView* control can display, insert, update, and delete records. The *FormView* control is more flexible but it's also more difficult to use. You have to supply an HTML template for each feature you want to use. If you'd like to see an example that uses the *FormView* control for adding records, inspect the secure/ProductAddFormView.aspx page in the sample files.

Table 15-1
DetailsView *Properties for the*
ProductAdd.aspx Page

Property	Setting	Description
AutoGenerateInsertButton	True	Specifies that the *DetailsView* control should display the controls for inserting database records.
AutoGenerateRows	False	Specifies that the *DetailsView* control shouldn't automatically display data-bound fields.
CssClass	formbox	Specifies a CSS class that formats the display.
DataKeyNames	ProductId	Specifies the list of fields that serve as the database table's primary key.
DataSourceId	SqlDataSource1	Specifies the name of the data source that updates the database.
DefaultMode	Insert	Specifies that the *DetailsView* control should remain in Insert mode after an Insert has occurred.
HorizontalAlign	center	Centers the *DetailsView* control within the available display space.

Figure 15-3 shows how the ProductAdd.aspx page looks in a browser. To add a Product record, the visitor would fill in a Category Id, Product Name, and Product Price, then click the Insert link.

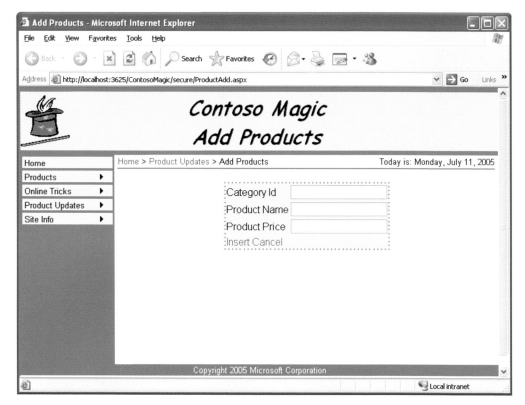

Figure 15-3
To add a database record by means of a DetailsView *control, the visitor types the new record values into the form fields and clicks the Insert link.*

If you like, you can put both the *GridView* control from the previous section and the *DetailsView* control from this section on the same Web page, and bind them both to the same data source.

As a practical matter, you should probably add both of the pages from this chapter to the Web.sitemap file so the site's menu system makes them easy to find. Chapter 17 will explain how to hide these menu items from visitors who don't have authority to run the pages.

In Summary...

With just a little additional configuration, a *GridView* control can not only display database records, but update and delete them as well. A *DetailsView* control can also insert records, but it only displays one record at a time.

The next chapter will explain how to publish a Microsoft® SQL Server™ database from your development site to a live production site.

Chapter 16

Publishing Your Database

When your Web site uses a database and you copy the site to another Web server, it's quite common to copy the database as well. In some cases, the two Web servers and the two database servers are so similar that the same database settings and the same file locations work in both sites without modification. If you find yourself in this situation, you probably won't need this chapter.

In a more common scenario, your development database server and your production database server will require different connection settings or different file locations, and you'll need to fix these settings on the production site. To do this, you'll need to know a little about Microsoft® SQL Server™, connection settings, and *connections strings* (which store those settings). This chapter will explain the basics.

Copying a SQL Server Database

Microsoft has simplified the task of copying SQL Server databases from one computer to another. In many cases, publishing a SQL Server database is just as easy as publishing a file-oriented database such as Microsoft Access. In no case, however, is it terribly difficult.

If all the following conditions are true, publishing your Web site and your database together is a very easy process.

- The source database runs on the same computer as the source Web site.

- The destination database runs on the same computer as the destination Web site.

- The source and destination database servers both support a new SQL Server 2005 feature called user instances, and that's the approach you plan to use.

You just publish the database files from the App_Data folder on the source site to the App_Data folder on the destination site. In any other case, the procedure is a little more complicated. Specifically, you'll need to:

1. Find out where your database files reside. To do this in Microsoft Visual Web Developer™:

    a. Open Database Explorer.

    b. Double-click any data connection that points to the database.

    c. In the Properties window, get the value of the Primary File Path property.

2. Stop your local copy of SQL Server. This ensures that SQL Server doesn't have exclusive control of the database files, and that all changes to the files are complete. To do this:

    a. Click Start, Programs, Microsoft SQL Server 2005, Configuration Tools, and SQL Configuration Manager.

    b. When the SQL Server Configuration Manager window appears, select SQL Server 2005 Services in the pane at the left.

    c. In the pane at the right, right-click SQL Server (SQLEXPRESS) and choose Stop from the shortcut menu.

Stopping the Windows service SQL Server (SQLEXPRESS) by any other means has the same effect. You can restart SQL Server after you've copied the files.

3. Copy the database's .mdf file (and .ldf file, if one exists) to the production database server. To get the exact location and the necessary upload procedure, ask your IT or Web host administrator.

4. Ask the administrator to attach the database files to a copy of SQL Server.

5. Obtain a connection string (or at least connection settings) from the administrator.

6. Install the new connection settings in the destination site's web.config file. A later section titled, "Using Connection Strings," will explain how to do this.

Among these steps, obtaining and then installing the new connection string are likely to be the most difficult. To do this successfully, you need to know something about database connection settings. To understand these settings, you need to know a little about SQL Server. The rest of this chapter explains what you need to know.

Understanding and Connecting to SQL Server

Microsoft SQL Server is an enterprise-class, industrial-strength database system. As such, it has a reputation for complexity. The deeper you delve into SQL Server, the more details you can discover.

Microsoft, however, is dedicated to ease of use and this includes SQL Server: Each release of SQL Server is more powerful, more reliable, more secure, and easier to use than the last. SQL Server 2005 continues this trend and SQL Server 2005 Express Edition expands upon it. Consider how smooth and natural it was to complete the examples in Chapters 13, 14, and 15, all of which used SQL Server Express.

SQL Server is a *network database*. This means that Web sites and other applications interact with SQL Server over *network connections*, rather than through the computer's file system. Figure 16-1 represents this schematically.

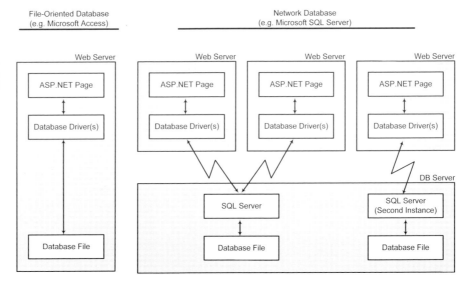

The configuration at the left is typical of file-oriented databases such as Microsoft Access. The *application* (or client) calls a database driver (or, more accurately, a *stack* of database drivers) and those drivers physically read and write the database file.

The configuration at the right illustrates a network database such as SQL Server. As before, the applications call the database driver. That driver, however, opens a network connection to a copy of SQL Server that runs as a background task on the same or another computer. SQL Server analyzes incoming requests, does the necessary work (including physical I/O), and sends any results back to the client computer.

Table 16-1 lists some of the most common top-level database drivers that support SQL Server. *Top-level* means that applications interface directly with these drivers.

Table 16-1
Microsoft Database Driver Technologies

Database Driver	Year Introduced	Description
ODBC	1992	Open Database Connectivity
OLE DB	1996	Object Linking and Embedding - Database
System.Data.SqlClient	2002	.NET Framework Data Provider for SQL Server

Using Connection Strings

The first step in using any database is to open a *database connection*. A series of parameters in a *connection string* tells the database driver which database to open, what kind of security to use, and what options should be in effect.

Visual Web Developer stores connection strings in an XML file named web.config. Here's a short but fairly typical example of this file. The connection string is the portion of line 5 shown in green. The line breaks are strictly for readability.

```
01 <?xml version="1.0" encoding="utf-8"?>
02 <configuration
03   xmlns="http://schemas.microsoft.com/.NetConfiguration/v2.0">
04   <connectionStrings>
05     <add name="ContosoMagicConnectionString"
          connectionString="Data Source=.\SQLEXPRESS;
        AttachDbFilename=|DataDirectory|\ContosoMagic.mdf;
        Integrated Security=True;
        User Instance=True"
06        providerName="System.Data.SqlClient" />
07   </connectionStrings>
08   <system.web>
09     <pages theme="" />
10   </system.web>
11 </configuration>
```

In this connection string:

- **Data Source** Specifies the name of the computer where SQL Server is running and, if necessary, an instance name. In the example, a period indicates the local computer and SQLEXPRESS is an *instance name*. (An instance name identifies a specific installation of SQL Server.)

- **AttachDbFilename** Specifies a database file that you want SQL Server to use. The expression |DataDirectory| means the Web site's App_Data folder, and ContosoMagic.mdf is the file that contains the SQL Server database.

- **Integrated Security=True** Specifies that when your Web suite connects to SQL server, it will log in using the Microsoft Windows® account that runs ASP.NET processes for your Web site. For the development Web server that comes with Visual Web Developer, this is the account you used when you logged into Windows.

- **User Instance=True** Specifies that you want SQL Server to start a new *instance* of itself (that is, a new running copy) just for your Web site. This instance will run under the Windows account of the process that requested it: that is, under the account that runs ASP.NET processes for your Web site.

Note that Integrated Security is a client setting and User Instance is a server setting. If both of these settings are True:

- The SQL client and the user instance of SQL Server will run under the same Windows account (which, on the development Web server, is yours).

- The user instance of SQL Server will have no more (and no fewer) privileges than the account that runs ASP.NET process for your Web site.

- Your Web site will have SQL Server administrator privileges within the user instance of SQL Server.

Connection strings of this type are very common on *development* computers running both Visual Web Developer and SQL Server Express. The connection string below is one of several formats common on *production* Web servers. This string would replace the portion of your Web.config file previously shown in green.

```
Data Source=sawbox; Initial Catalog=ContosoMagic; User Id=presto; Password=chango;
```

As to the parameters:

- **Data Source** Specifies the name of the computer where SQL Server is running; if an instance name had been required, the parameter value would have been sawbox\ *instance*.

- **Initial Catalog** Specifies the name of an existing database. This is a logical name and not a physical file name. SQL Server "remembers" which physical files contain each logical database.

- **User Id** Provides a username for opening the database.

- **Password** Provides a password for opening the database.

This connection string doesn't specify *AttachDbFilename* and a filename because an administrator previously created the database or permanently attached an .mdf file. It doesn't specify *Integrated Security=True* because the administrator configured SQL Server to use its own user id and password system. The *User Id* and *Password* parameters specify those values.

If the administrator wanted SQL Server client applications to present Windows accounts as credentials, the connection string would look like this:

```
Data Source=sawbox; Initial Catalog=ContosoMagic; Integrated Security=True;
```

The administrator would also configure SQL Server so the account that runs ASP.NET processes for your Web site has access to the necessary databases.

Table 16-2 summarizes the most common parameters that appear in SQL Server connection strings. You don't have to memorize all of these, but you *should* keep this list handy and remember that connection strings provide settings for opening a database.

> **NOTE**
> When Table 16-2 groups two or more parameter names into one table row, those parameter names are equivalent.

Table 16-2
SQL Server Connection String
Parameters

Parameter	Description
Data Source, Server, Address, Addr, Network Address	The computer name or network address of the SQL Server that manages your database. Values set to *(local)* or a period (.) indicate the local computer.
Network Library, Net	The network library that the client computer will use when communicating with SQL Server. In essence, this determines the communication mode. Table 16-3 lists the supported values. Note that any library you choose must be present on both the client and server computers, and that the network connecting them must support the given protocol. If you specify a local server—for example, by coding *(local)* or a period (.)—and don't specify a network library, the default is shared memory. Otherwise, the default is dbmssocn (TCP/IP).
Database, Initial Catalog	The logical name of the database.
AttachDbFilename, Extended Properties, Initial File Name	The name of the primary .mdf file, including the full path name, of an attachable database. If you also specify the *Database* parameter, that value will become the logical name of the database you attach. Otherwise, SQL Server will use the file name base and extension as the database name.

Continued on next page

Continued from page 180

Parameter	Description
Integrated Security, *Trusted_Connection*	When *false*, you must code the *User ID* and *Password* parameters with the identify of a SQL Server account that has permission to open your database. This is the default. The values *false* and *no* are equivalent.
	When *true*, SQL Server will base permissions on the Windows account that runs ASP.NET processes for your Web site. The values *true*, *yes,* and *sspi* are equivalent.
User Id	The SQL Server login account. Code this parameter only if Integrated Security is *false*.
Password, *Pwd*	The SQL Server login account password. Code this parameter only if Integrated Security is *false*.
User Instance	If *true*, SQL Server will create a new instance of itself to service the connection. That instance will run under the client computer's Windows login account, but treat that account as a SQL Server administrator.
	The default is *false*.

Library	Name	Description
*l*dbnmpntw	Named Pipes	Windows networking
dbmsrpcn	Multiprotocol	Windows RPC
dbmsadsn	Apple Talk	Apple Datastream Protocol (ADSP)
dbmslpcn	Shared Memory	Process-to-process within one computer
dbmsspxn	IPX/SPX	Novell Netware
dbmssocn	TCP/IP	Internet sockets

Table 16-3
SQL Server Network Libraries

Sharing a Single Copy of SQL Server

Multiple applications, running on any combination of computers, can connect to SQL Server and use its capabilities simultaneously. This is one of the reasons SQL Server can handle much heavier loads than a file-oriented database system. If two or more applications submit conflicting requests—perhaps attempting to update the same record—SQL Server arbitrates these conflicts much more efficiently than a file-oriented database like Access.

Administering Shared SQL Servers

When several applications or development groups use the same copy of SQL Server, it's quite normal for none of them to have Administrator privileges. This keeps the applications (or development groups) secure from each other.

In shared environments, a database administrator (DBA) usually receives requests for new databases, security changes, backups, restores, and other tasks from developers, verifies their authenticity, and then performs the work. This means, of course, that the developers must submit service requests and wait for the DBA to complete them. The DBA typically works in the IT department or at a hosting company.

Server Instances

A single computer can run several *instances* (that is, *copies*) of SQL Server. A server instance is a stand-alone copy of SQL Server, independent of any other instances on the same computer. For example, each instance could be a different version. Each instance runs as its own Windows service. An administrator creates server instances by running SQL Server Setup for each one. Each server instance on the same computer has a different *instance name*.

In Figure 16-1, two applications are accessing the first instance of SQL Server, and one application is accessing the second instance. However, each copy of SQL Server is a full server instance. If the need arose, either could service dozens or hundreds of applications at once.

User Instances

SQL Server 2005 and SQL Server Express both support a new kind of SQL Server instancing: *user instances*. When an application requests a user instance, SQL Server:

- Loads a new copy of itself into memory.
- Runs the new instance with that application's Windows logon account. (For an ASP.NET Web site, this is the account that runs the site's ASP.NET processes.)
- Grant's the application's logon account Administrator permissions, but only within that instance.
- Terminates the instance after a period of inactivity.

If you create a database in Visual Web Developer, if a Web site is open, and if SQL Server 2005 or SQL Server Express is running on the same machine, then Visual Web Developer will:

- Ask SQL Server to start a user instance.
- Use that instance to create that database, locating its files in the site's App_Data folder.
- Configure the site to request a user instance whenever it opens the database.

This is a very useful approach because it gives you, as the Web developer, permission to create databases and perform other administrative tasks with no security restrictions. However, because the user instance is running under the same Windows logon account as your Web site, it can't access, modify, or administer databases that belong to other sites.

When SQL Server is running as a user instance, the following limitations are in effect:

- Automatic replication is unavailable.
- SQL Server usernames and passwords are unavailable. You must use Windows authentication.
- The network protocol must be local named pipes (that is, shared memory). This is automatic, but means the client and server must run on the same computer.
- A user instance shares the registry entries of the server instance that created it.

- You must access the database through ADO.NET. Code that Visual Web Developer creates through its graphical interface always satisfies this requirement. Older programs that use ODBC or OLE DB will fail.

Attaching Database Files

When you ask SQL Server to create a database, it must obtain disk space for storing the data. It does this by creating a file with an .mdf filename extension and then *attaching* that file to the new database. When you begin to use the database, SQL Server also creates a log file with an .ldf filename extension.

If you copy an .mdf file (and its companion .ldf file, if any), you can *attach* the copied files to any other instance of SQL Server. The SQL Server that attaches the .mdf and .ldf files can then deliver a copied version of the database to any application that needs it. There are two ways of attaching databases:

- Through administrative tools such as SQL Server Enterprise Manager or Microsoft Visual Studio®. This is the normal approach for shared copies of SQL Server.

- By using the *AttachDBFileName* connection string parameter. This is the normal approach for user instances.

Understanding Logins

Every copy of SQL Server verifies the identity of each client that attempts a connection and tries to access its resources. SQL Server uses this identity to determine what privileges the client has on the server as a whole, and also for each of the server's databases. Two very different types of accounts are valid for this purpose:

- **Windows Accounts** Every process on every Windows computer runs under a Windows login account. On Internet Information Server (IIS), for example, many Web sites use a local account named IUSR_*computername* for non-ASP.NET processes. In addition:
  - On IIS 5.0 ASP.NET processes run by default under a local account named ASP.NET.
  - On IIS 6.0, ASP.NET processes run by default under a local account named Network Services.

Despite these defaults, an administrator can configure any Web site to run under any suitably-configured Windows account (local or domain).

If your connection string specifies *Integrated Security=true* or *Trusted_Connection=true*, SQL Server will determine the site's database privileges based on the Windows account the site uses to run ASP.NET processes.

Note that if IIS and SQL Server are running on different machines, this Windows account must be a domain account, and the two servers need to be in the same or trusting domains. A local account on the IIS machine wouldn't be valid on the SQL Server machine, and vice versa.

■ **SQL Server Accounts** If an administrator decides it isn't practical to set up Windows accounts for every Web site (or perhaps for every virtual server), the administrator can choose to use SQL Server accounts instead.

These accounts exist solely within a single copy of SQL Server. They have nothing do with Windows login accounts or Active Directory® directory service. A caution: because they use less encryption, they're not as secure as Windows accounts.

If your connection string specifies (or defaults to) *Integrated Security=false* or its equivalent, *Trusted_Connection=false*, it must also contain *User Id=* and *Password=* parameters to specify the SQL Server username and password.

How Visual Web Developer Uses SQL Server

Microsoft has tried very hard to ensure that you never encounter security problems while developing Web sites on your own computer. As a result, on a Windows computer running Visual Web Developer and SQL Server Express:

■ The development Web server runs under the Windows account you logged in with.

■ The Windows account that installed SQL Server Express (probably yours) will be an administrator on that copy of SQL Server Express.

- All your connection strings will default to *Integrated Security=true*.

- Even if you didn't install the computer's copy of SQL Server Express, you can get SQL Server administrative rights by requesting a *user instance* in your connection string. The section, *"User Instances,"* earlier in this chapter explained how this works.

If, however, you're using a centrally-managed and shared SQL Server for development (or, even more likely, on your production site) then you may need to adjust your connection strings to fit your environment. A previous section in this chapter, "Using Connection Strings," explained how to do this.

In Summary...

With the introduction of Visual Web Developer and SQL Server Express, Microsoft has made using SQL Server as easy as using file-oriented databases like Microsoft Access.

If the source and destination database servers both support user instances, you can simply publish your SQL Server database files with the rest of your Web site.

If not, just copy your database files where the destination database administrator instructs you, and then configure the destination Web site's connection parameters accordingly.

The next chapter will explain how to identify your Web visitors, how to protect parts of your site from unauthorized visitors, and how to remember settings and preferences for each identified visitor.

Index

A

absolute positioning, 64–65
access. See also security
databases, 138
AccessDataSource data source control, 151
accounts
SQL Server, 185
Windows Accounts, 184–185
Add Connection dialog box, 139–141
Add New Item dialog box, 86, 117
Add New Item page, 52–53
Add Style Rule command (Styles menu), 110
Add Style Rule dialog box, 110
Add WHERE Clause dialog box
administration
database access, 138
shared SQL Servers, 182
Advanced command (Edit menu), 82
Advanced setting (Select Statement dialog box), 153
Anonymous Login field (Choose Location dialog box), 33
App_Data folder, 142
copy SQL Server databases, 174–175
copying, 48
applications
IIS, 24
master pages, 103–106
looking inside master pages, 104
modification of existing pages, 104–105
modification of header information, 106
relative URLs, 106
Microsoft Visual Web Developer 2005 Express Edition, 3–4
user controls, 90–93
coding attributes, 92–93
CSS styles, 91
relative URLs, 91–92

tags, 90
Visual Web Developer 2005 Express Edition, 3–4
Web user controls, CSS styles, 91
arbitrary Web sites, opening, 37–43
ASP.NET 2.0
data format strings, 161–162
features, 1–2
Literal controls, 10
programming model, 13
resources, 3
server controls, 14–16, 20
themes, 115–123
adding CSS style sheets, 119–120
adding skins, 116–119
applying to Web pages and sites, 120–123
creating, 116
Web page delivery, 14–19
events, 18–19
hierarchy of controls, 16–17
page life cycle, 19
Web site hyperlinks
breadcrumbs, 134–136
drop-down menus, 131–133
fly-out menus, 131–133
site map files, 126–130
Tree View menus, 133–134
ASP.NET Development Server, 24
ASP.NET Web Matrix, 5
AttachDbFilename, Extended Properties, Initial File Name parameter, 180
AttachDbFileName connection string, 184
attaching database files, 184
attributes, coding, Web user controls, 92–93
Auto Format command (control shortcut menus), 63
AutoGenerateInsertButton property (DetailsView control), 170

AutoGenerateRows property (DetailsView control), 170
AutoPostBack="True" attribute (server controls), 22

B

bannertxt CSS rule, 99
Bookmark All command (Find and Replace command), 78
bookmarks, source code text editor, 72
Bookmarks command (Edit menu), 72
bordertext CSS rule, 100
bordertxt CSS rule, 98
BoundField properties, 161
breadcrumbs, linking Web site pages, 134–136
Build menu commands, Build Web Site, 83
Build Web Site command (Build menu), 83

C

C#, resources, 3
Cascading Style Sheets. See CSS
categorization, server controls, 20
Web custom controls, 20–21
Web user controls, 20
CategoryId field (Products table), 145
centralized page layout, master pages, 95–96
Change Data Source dialog box, 139
child instances. See user instances
Choose Data Source dialog box, 139
Choose Data Source option, 169
Choose Location dialog box, 28–29
Choose Name dialog box, 145
Choose Your Data Connection dialog box, 151–152
Class Selector (CSS style names), 110
Code Behind progam code storage, 82
code completion. See IntelliSense

What do you think of this book?
We want to hear from you!

Do you have a few minutes to participate in a brief online survey? Microsoft is interested in hearing your feedback about this publication so that we can continually improve our books and learning resources for you.

To participate in our survey, please visit:
www.microsoft.com/learning/booksurvey

And enter this book's ISBN, 0-7356-2212-4. As a thank-you to survey participants in the United States and Canada, each month we'll randomly select five respondents to win one of five $100 gift certificates from a leading online merchant.* At the conclusion of the survey, you can enter the drawing by providing your email address, which will be used for prize notification only.

Thanks in advance for your input. Your opinion counts!

Sincerely,

Microsoft Learning

Learn More. Go Further.

To see special offers on Microsoft Learning products for developers, IT professionals, and home and office users, visit:
www.microsoft.com/learning/booksurvey